WITHDRAWN

Hyères, 24 July 57

Edition Peters 6269

THE ARTISTIC LEGACY
OF WALT WHITMAN

A Tribute to
Gay Wilson Allen

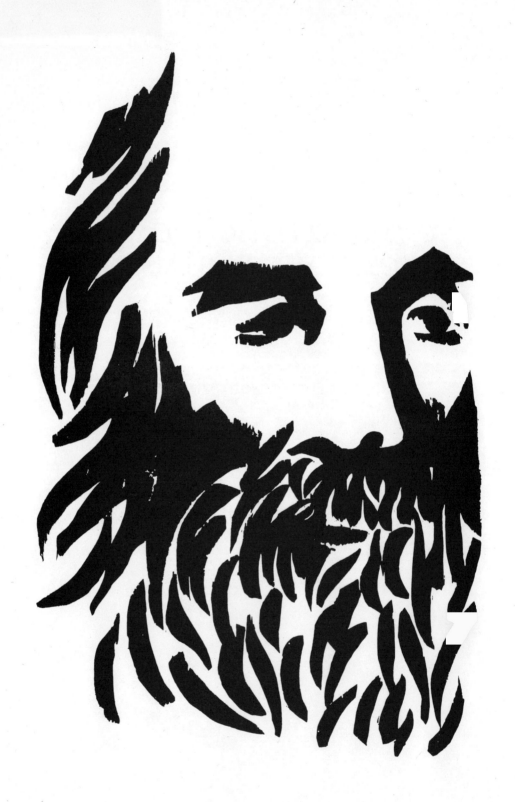

THE ARTISTIC LEGACY
OF WALT WHITMAN

A Tribute to
Gay Wilson Allen

Edited by EDWIN HAVILAND MILLER

1970

NEW YORK UNIVERSITY PRESS

© 1970 BY NEW YORK UNIVERSITY
LIBRARY OF CONGRESS CATALOG CARD NUMBER: 71–111520
MANUFACTURED IN THE UNITED STATES OF AMERICA

Foreword

*A Walt Whitman Celebration was
held at New York University from
April 13 to 25, 1969, to commemorate
the 150th anniversary of the poet's
birth. The final speaker was the "dean"
of Whitman scholars, Gay Wilson Allen.
At the conclusion of Professor Allen's
address, "The Iconography of Walt
Whitman," Professor Edwin Haviland
Miller made the following
presentation:*

I should like to make a few relevant remarks—and when I use that abused word, "relevant," it is not modish gibberish—for these remarks will be relevant to the conclusion of this Walt Whitman Celebration and relevant to the conclusion of Gay Wilson Allen's active career at New York University. I am to have the pleasure but also the sorrow of attempting to render publicly the respect and fondness I have for Gay Wilson Allen.

Gay is a gentle man. Gentle men are not in fashion in these days of strident confrontations and ear-shattering shrieks, too often filled with self-hatred and too seldom warmed by love of and respect for human dignity and humane values. Whitman was a rebel and an iconoclast, and he was a "problem" to the nineteenth-century establishment. But he wrote his "barbaric yawp" with a wit seldom shared by the Puritans of the atomic age, and he never clothed his (admittedly inconsistent) convictions in a self-righteous straitjacket. For, despite his rhetoric and his occasional bombast, Whitman was a gentle man—a man of sensitive, delicate temperament, of abiding faith in democracy and mankind.

His definitive biographer, in the best Whitmanesque tradition, has not pronounced finalities of egomaniacal certitude, but has patiently, carefully, and tentatively attempted to explain the complexities of a poet who delighted in his contradictions and who deliberately confused his future interpreters through his skillful manipulations of his public image.

As a gentle man, Gay Wilson Allen quietly taught thousands of students here at New York University, both at the University Heights and the Washington Square campuses. Into his classroom he brought warmth, humor, creative insight, a flexible mind, and an intelligence enriched by research.

I realize that I am but feebly expressing the gratitude of these students, particularly the graduate students, who learned the values and restraints of responsible scholarship. Gay represents what appears to be under attack by those who want shortcuts to academic distinction without the pains (and they are great) but also the gratifications (and they are also great) of creative and dedicated scholarship.

Gay has wedded teaching and research, and it has been a most successful marriage—in the best traditions of American education, which has done some things, despite its critics, superlatively well.

Gay is too modest, as becomes a gentle man, to tell people how well known he and his writings on Whitman are in Japan, India, and Europe. He will not tell you how many young people have come from other countries to study with him at New York University or to consult with him about their Whitman studies. Nor will he mention how generously he has given of himself to the Whitmanites as well as to the Whitmaniacs.

I have had two mentors. In my graduate years and those immediately following, I worked with another gentle man, Professor Hyder Rollins, who gave of himself to his students with a generosity that seems all the more surprising when one recalls that he published forty-five books. When in the early 1950s I stumbled upon Walt Whitman and became an Elizabethan gone right, Hyder Rollins warned me, but without reproach, that I would become a scholar in American literature.

Then it was that I met my second mentor, Gay Wilson Allen. Probably no one has read *The Solitary Singer* as often as I have—except, of course, Gay and Evie. Probably no one has enjoyed as I have the warmth

and gracious assistance of Gay Wilson Allen. So in the deepest sense I
stand here tonight as a student of a mentor who did that student the
highest honor of recommending that he become a colleague at New York
University.

For over two years Gay and I have worked together in arranging
this celebration. For over two years I have indulged, like Whitman, but
unlike Gay, in "faint clews & indirections" in deceiving him, in keeping
from him a secret well known to a few others. As he knows, the lectures
in this celebration, including the one you have just heard, are to be
collected and published by New York University Press.

What follows Gay does not know:

*I herewith name that book THE ARTISTIC LEGACY OF WALT
WHITMAN.*

*I herewith dedicate that book to Gay Wilson Allen. The subtitle
will read: "A Tribute to Gay Wilson Allen."*

*Finally—and like Whitman's "finallies," this finally is but a new
beginning—I present that book as a token of the affection of his students,
his colleagues, and the University—to one of the most esteemed and
beloved teacher-scholars of our day.*

Acknowledgments

ELIZABETH BISHOP

CHARLES E. FEINBERG

ANTONIO FRASCONI

PROFESSOR DAVID H. GREENE

MR. AND MRS. BEN HELLER

SIDNEY JANIS GALLERY

TONY KEYS

LIBRARY OF CONGRESS

MRS. HORATIO GATES LLOYD

MARLBOROUGH-GERSON GALLERY

THE METROPOLITAN MUSEUM OF ART

ROBERT MOTHERWELL

THE MUSEUM OF MODERN ART

RARE BOOK DIVISION, THE NEW YORK PUBLIC LIBRARY

PROFESSOR FRANCIS V. O'CONNOR

THE PENNSYLVANIA ACADEMY OF THE FINE ARTS

RARE BOOK DEPARTMENT, THE UNIVERSITY OF PENNSYLVANIA LIBRARY

EDWARD P. SHINMAN

DEAN GEORGE WINCHESTER STONE, JR.

UNITED STATES ARMY SIGNAL CORPS

SAM WAGSTAFF

WALT WHITMAN HOUSE, CAMDEN, NEW JERSEY

THE WHITNEY MUSEUM OF AMERICAN ART

CONTENTS

List of Illustrations

Frontispiece: Woodcut by Antonio Frasconi (1969).

1. Barnett Newman, "Abraham" (1949).
   Collection The Museum of Modern Art, New York, Philip Johnson Fund.

2. Robert Motherwell, "Chi ama, crede" (1962).
   Collection of the artist.

3. David Smith, "Hudson River Landscape" (1951), welded steel.
   Whitney Museum of American Art. Photograph: Geoffrey Clements.

4. Claes Oldenburg, "Giant Good Humor" (1965), mixed media.
   Courtesy Sidney Janis Gallery, New York. Photograph: Geoffrey Clements.

5. Jackson Pollock, "Male and Female" (1942).
   Collection of Mrs. Horatio Gates Lloyd, Haverford, Pa. Photograph: Alfred J. Wyatt.

6. Jackson Pollock, "Autumn Rhythm" (1950).
   The Metropolitan Museum of Art, George A. Hearn Fund, 1957.

7. Jackson Pollock, "Blue Poles," (1953).
   Collection Mr. and Mrs. Ben Heller, New York. Photograph: The Museum of Modern Art.

8. Jackson Pollock, "The Deep" (1953).
   Collection Sam Wagstaff, Detroit. Photograph: Marlborough-Gerson Gallery.

9. Walt Whitman, daguerreotype (1840?).
   Walt Whitman House, Camden, New Jersey.

10. Walt Whitman, daguerreotype (1854), "the Christ likeness."
    Walt Whitman House, Camden, New Jersey.

Oscar Cargill

Gay Wilson Allen:
A Tribute

1.

The preference of presidents, boards of trustees, and philanthropists for building with stone, concrete, and steel over building with men is easily understood: they erect something visible and permanent rather than something intangible and transient as the most brilliant faculty ever assembled. Indeed, whenever a department is designated as outstanding, it has passed its apogee and is already on the decline.

Immediately after World War II, when it became incumbent upon the Department of English at New York University to find somebody, anybody, to fill a vacancy in American literature in University College and the Graduate School, I found myself on a "search" committee for a "replacement." It was my first assignment of this sort, and I am certain that I took it more seriously than my similarly assigned colleagues, who were all in English literature and to whom the appointment of a man in the "upstart subject" could not have been a thing of too much importance. Further, I knew exactly whom I wanted, which is an immense advantage for one on a committee that has no candidates. Unfortunately my man would have, in the eyes of my colleagues, two serious limitations: he was presently teaching in a small Midwestern state university recently created from a minor school of education, and he had just finished a book on Walt Whitman, that moral miscreant, whom he had treated with a respect that they would accord only to a Milton or a Wordsworth. How I overcame the first of these shortcomings I cannot recall: possibly I extolled his knowledge of prosody and criticism as evidences of scholarship; more probably I simply "bullied" my colleagues, for despite an inward timidity and self-doubt which I have never overcome, I had developed the arrogant persona of an autocrat which I learned to exploit to advantage in the publishing and academic worlds. The second obstacle I avoided completely. This, to the best of my recollection, is the authentic history of the appointment of Gay Wilson Allen to the faculties of New York University.

But it is not the end of the tale. I have, and had, two very strong convictions about the necessary qualifications of a university professor: the first is that he should be a *proved* scholar, and the second is that he should be an excellent teacher. My own reading had satisfied me that Professor Allen was at that moment the best man in American literature not attached to a large university. The validity of my assumption in this regard was shortly satisfied by an offer to him from Western Reserve University after he had accepted the proposal we made him. That second offer originated with Professor Lyon Richardson, one of the few great readers in our field. I used my connection with a national publishing house to get its representative in that area to discover whether my candidate was a good classroom teacher and a congenial colleague. I had the warmest assurances on both scores.

Professor Allen's acceptance of our offer proved to me that it was possible to build at New York University an English department of some excellence, and, as a result of my experience on the search committee, which left me somewhat doubtful, I confess, of the competence of my colleagues to achieve this, I secretly and brashly resolved to accomplish it myself. The vanity of this ambition I will not defend, but it is only fair to the testator to state that it was the absolute definition of that ambition, too. Shortly I was a member of a triumvirate which advised the head of the department, who was in failing health, and, within three years, I was chairman of the department at Washington Square with the budget in my control. The headship came later.

With Gay Allen as my cornerstone and model, and with a great deal of good luck, in the next seventeen years I altered the process of search for an English faculty, obtained more money to attract good men, and succeeded, after a fashion, in creating a passably good department.

II.

One of the true values of being chairman is the rare privilege of choosing your friends, not having them thrust upon you by chance. I suppose I never consciously added a man to the department because I liked him, but I invariably chose persons because I liked the articles or books they had written. I was entranced by their minds. One of the real afflictions of this life is having to endure the pretentiousness of mediocrity, the kind of mediocrity one finds in colleges. If the executive officer of a department has to put up with much of this, he has no one to blame but himself: he has not inquired deeply enough into the character of the candidate as revealed by his writing. Interviews and meetings with the members of the department have their place, but a plausible fellow fares better than an able scholar in such encounters, whereas a man expresses himself indelibly in what he writes. It is laborious to read down a man, that is, read him down to the extent that you can gain a notion, not merely of his scholarly competence, but of his character. A chairman owes it to his colleagues to protect them from the aggressive, the quick-tempered, the unstable, the unreliable. He should be as quick to detect "phoniness" as was Holden Caulfield. If a man writes enough (and you want only a "productive" man), he soon reveals who he is and what he is. Another way, of course, is to choose a good man first, and match your later choices against him. I had Gay Wilson Allen.

Gay was immediately my friend, and it was a friendship in which I was the greater recipient of beneficence. I had done some minor work on Whitman, but just enough to realize the thoroughness of Gay's possession and the balance of his judgment of that not easily compassed poet—let no one think that Gay ever derived the slightest usable hint from me in our many conversations on Whitman. In fact, though I think he expanded his knowledge and came upon new materials, his attitude was established and mature by the time he had finished the *Walt Whitman Handbook* (1946)—the book that first captured my attention. What a substantial piece of scholarship it is, and what a guide through the chaos of Whitman's writing and thinking! Gay was the first to put in clear definition the differences between the editions of *Leaves of Grass* in Whitman's lifetime. He was the first to examine the text minutely and to demonstrate that conscious poetic improvement was an achieved end of Whitman's revisions. Any great writer tests out a critic, but Whitman more than most—iconoclastic both in substance and form, he provokes extremes of statement from both admirers and contemners. I was attracted to Gay's examination of Whitman's life and work in the *Handbook* by its dispassionate objectivity and, to borrow a phrase, its "sweet reasonableness." I found these to be traits of the author's own character.

Of course, I had read the earlier books before presenting his name to the search committee. His *American Prosody* (1935) is a properly titled book, for his is a pioneer investigation of the features of American poetic composition, which is as different from British versifying as American speech is from British speech. "His voice alone is Eliot," Stephen Spender remarks; Eliot could change his church and his country, but he was quite unable to change his native rhythms, a thing so subtle few American commentators would note it. Gay's book is a study of the techniques and rhythms of eleven Americans, beginning with Philip Freneau and ending with Emily Dickinson. *Literary Criticism: Pope to Croce* (1941), which he edited with Harry Hayden Clark, the distinguished Wisconsin scholar, is a very good anthology of literary criticism. My own taste is less cautious and more ranging, but the student who lives with this anthology will have a substantial knowledge of what preceded the "New Criticism," that critical upheaval which occurred at the beginning of the thirties. I had had occasion to use *Thirty-five Years of Whitman Bibliography: 1918–1942* (1943) before Gay's advent and found it one of those useful books rarely hymned by the reviewers, though celebrated in library journals. The Bibliographical Society issued *Walt Whitman's Reception in Scandinavia* (1946) in the same year as the *Handbook;* it looks forward to *Walt Whitman Abroad* (1955), a collection of essays from critics all over the world, Whitman having found disciples in such widely separated places as western Russia and India, Spain and Japan.

Given a seminar in Whitman, alternating with a Melville seminar, Gay attracted graduate students from ever-expanding circles of influence. Because we have the practice at New York University, not common everywhere, of giving undergraduates a look at our stars, he reached and converted to American literature a wide range of students. The devotion of neophytes and of graduate students alike, for he enjoyed the respect of all, was a joy to witness. His wise tolerance and quiet humor spread a balm in the department and encouraged imitation. One of the quietest of men and the least obtrusive, he was showered with invitations to speak and spread the reception and fame of Whitman well beyond the academic walls. The summit of his fame as a lecturer was reached when he was invited to talk on "Whitman, the Man" by the Library of Congress under the auspices of the Gertrude Clarke Whittall Poetry and Literature Fund. Later he was to become a founder and a trustee of the Walt Whitman Birthplace Association; and on May 31, 1969, the one hundred and fiftieth anniversary of the poet's birth, the Association presented Gay Wilson Allen with a plaque commemorating his services to Whitman scholarship.

Gay was not only the principal speaker on the occasion but also the guest editor of *The Long-Islander*, a newspaper founded by Walt Whitman in 1838.

Masters of American Literature (1949), an anthology which he edited with Henry Pochmann of the University of Wisconsin, demonstrated his broad acquaintance with the subject. All things led to *The Solitary Singer: A Critical Biography of Walt Whitman* in 1955. I surrender the phrase "the definitive life" to the blurb writers, who have exhausted its meaning. Suffice it to say that there is no rival for this book and the prospect is dim that it will be seriously challenged for a long time. It did not get the Pulitzer Prize for biography in the year it was published; as I remember it, that reward went to a minor historian writing on a minor figure, who has since passed into utter oblivion. Nevertheless *The Solitary Singer* won the Taminent Award as "the best biography of the year"—which it was. Indeed, how thoroughly is the life of Whitman treated in this book: the nobility of the hospital service in the War, the absurdity of the Anne Gilchrist pursuit, the dubiety of the Peter Doyle relationship, the devotion of fast friends such as Burroughs, Traubel, and O'Connor, the cautious approval of some of the Pre-Raphaelites and the bold endorsement of Emerson, the physically defective ancestry, the improbable journalistic and political adventures, the filial and fraternal loyalties, the calm fronting of evening, paralysis, and death—all receive the most thorough examination and discussion. The writing is more than good, it is lively and varied, and its tone is frequently that of detached amusement. The author has captured his subject, not the subject the author.

In the same year that he produced *The Solitary Singer*, Professor Allen edited a volume of selected *Poems* of Walt Whitman with Charles Davis (now of Pennsylvania State University, but then an instructor in the department). He had written a doctoral thesis on Edwin Arlington Robinson under Gay's direction. Because the pair honored me with a dedication, I am disqualified from judging this book, but secretly hold it to be of a superior excellence.

Also in 1955 Gay Allen formulated plans for the first scholarly and authoritative edition of the poet's works, and personally selected the editors for the various volumes. The first two volumes, *The Correspondence of Walt Whitman, 1842–1875*, edited by Gay's colleague, Edwin Haviland Miller, appeared in 1961. *The Collected Writings of Walt Whitman* is a major publishing undertaking of New York University

Press, and, when completed, will be the outstanding memorial to Whitman as an author.

As if to demonstrate that *The Solitary Singer*, despite its thoroughness, had not exhausted his knowledge of Whitman, Gay contributed a *Walt Whitman* (1961) to the Evergreen Profile Series and in the same year published *Walt Whitman as Man, Poet, and Legend*. The former, intended for a popular audience, is handsomely illustrated, with many unusual portraits of the poet, his family, and his friends, with an accompanying depiction of places he frequented, portions of manuscript, and the like; the latter includes a most valuable "Check List of Whitman Publications 1945–1960" by Gay's wife, Evie Allison Allen, an expert bibliographer and translator. In 1965, with Professors Walter B. Rideout and James K. Robinson, Professor Allen compiled an anthology of the best American poetry, beginning with Anne Bradstreet and ending with Wendell Berry, recently head of freshman English in University College and now a poet of stature.

Hardly tired of Whitman, indeed still indefatigably in pursuit of him through *The Collected Writings*, Gay began gathering materials for a life of William James in the late fifties. Strangely, aside from Ralph Barton Perry's *The Thought and Character of William James* (1935), which is more a study of the sources of James's psychology and philosophy than a life of the Harvard thinker, there was no full biography of James. Gay was more than half persuaded in his choice of subject by Leon Edel, who, in his work on William's brother Henry, had discovered how much material existed and was instrumental in making it available. Expert now in evaluating what he looked at, diligent in searching out the best, and writing swiftly and with ease, Gay produced a mammoth manuscript, which, on the advice of his publisher, he reduced to a volume comparable to *The Solitary Singer*. This was published in 1967 as *William James: A Biography*. Wisely eschewing the approach that Perry had effectively exploited, Gay concentrated on the living William James, stressing neither the psychologist nor the philosopher, but rather the man in his complex family and social relationships. It is the history of a strong personality that set in vibration a whole generation of American men and women. The author responded to his subject as Harvard undergraduates responded to Professor James. The result is a thoroughly fleshed figure of the warmest blooded man of the turn of the century, a genuinely intrepid spirit. The *William James* is selling as I write. It should long continue to do so, for how, will a prize committee tell me, can one write a better biography?

Although not due to retire for several years, Gay Wilson Allen has decided to cease teaching in order to devote himself to writing. Gay leaves us to accept an offer of a final term at Harvard, but that is merely a kind of laureateship. His real purpose is to add a third volume, as I have intimated, to what is to be a trilogy of hope and faith. He has brought order to the career of the most chaotic figure in American literature in his biography of Whitman, he has "steadied down" the most volatile philosopher among philosophers in his life of William James, and now he approaches the mystery and contradictions of Ralph Waldo Emerson, whom each man claimed as a master. I shall venture no predictions as to the outcome of his latest undertaking, for they would embarrass Gay, who prefers to say with characteristic self-effacement, "I just try."

Ned Rorem

Words Without Song

(Notes on the Poetry of Music)

If the arts inherently expressed or even resembled each other, we would need only one. Still, more often than they are differentiated they are likened. The most frequent comparison is made between music and architecture, though these are the most dissimilar.

Music serves no purpose beyond itself, and the identifying property of that self is motion. Architecture does serve a purpose beyond itself, and its identifying property is static. Architecture would thus seem closer to painting or sculpture, while music—as flow—obviously resembles dance, or even prose. Yet unlike prose, or even dance, music has no innate content, no symbolic sense. If a building has symbolic sense, the primary function is nonetheless practical. An architect cannot improvise a plan and the plan's execution as he goes along the way artists can, for their work is not useful. An architect who omits a beam will see his structure collapse, if he overlooks a bathroom the tenants collapse. When artists fail, no one but themselves really gets hurt.

Music then inhabits an opposite pole from architecture, with prose and painting falling somewhere between.

❋ ❋ ❋

If music lacks content beyond itself, can it then be compared with poetry? "What does it *mean?*" people hopelessly ask of a poem. About music they do not ask *why*—at least not in the sense of its dealing a double standard, of being beauty that instructs. When singers question me on the significance of the words to a song, I answer easily: "They signify whatever my music tells you they signify. What more do I know about poetry?"

Poems are not Why. They are Because. Comprised of both question and answer, they mirror music more singularly than any other human enterprise. Perhaps because of their common quality, poetry and music often marry. Now the marriages, however seemingly ideal to outsiders, are all based on misunderstanding at best, at worst on total perversion.

❋   ❋   ❋

Having his verse set to music is not necessarily the ultimate compliment a poet may receive from a composer. Yet many poets today covet the idea, at least before the fact. They ponder Beethoven and Schiller, Schumann and Heine, Ravel and Mallarmé, those sublime collaborative unions wherein the poets' words were illuminated while presumably remaining the same—the same, only more so! Actually those unions were not collaborations at all. They were settings of a *fait accompli*, the *fait* being verse able to stand alone, the *accompli* being a denial of that ability, resulting not in "the poem only more so" but in a transformation: a song. The song often bemused the poet who, though perhaps pleased (more likely dismayed), never quite recognized his original impulse. After all, had he not heard his own "music" while composing the poem? Naturally no musician hears that poem the same way, or why would he write a song?

Song is a reincarnation. Poetry must be destroyed in order to live again in music. A composer, no matter how respectful, must treat poetry as a skeleton on which to bestow flesh, breaking a few bones in the process. He does not render a poem more *musical* (poetry is not music, it is poetry); he weds it to sound, creating a third entity of different and sometimes greater magnitude than either of its parents. It too may ultimately stand alone, as those nineteenth-century songs now do, although they were disowned at birth by their poetic fathers. *We* hear them as totalities without considering their growing pains.

Indeed, much past poetry is known to us exclusively through song settings; hence our unconscious assumption of such poetry's emanations of musical inevitability. Yet when it comes to his own work, today's poet has his own notion of inevitability. Wanting to have his cake and eat it, he is torn between a need to hear his words sung and a desire for those words to retain their initial beat and echo, their identity proper. His "proper" must obligatorily be sacrificed; his notion of inevitability becomes the fly in the ointment. The only inevitable way to set poetry is the "right" way, and there is no one right way.

Song is the sole example in which one pre-existing art medium is juxta-posed intact upon another. The words of the poem are not *adapted*, like film scenarios from plays; they remain unaltered while being tampered with, and unlike other musical forms—fugue, for instance, or sonata—there exist no fixed rules for creating a song. (The so-called "A-B-A structure" of Tin Pan Alley or folk tunes is unrelated to the necessary freedom of the so-called "art song," and it is actually more frequently encountered in instrumental movements.)

There are as many "right" ways for tampering with a poem as there are poems and good composers, or different viewpoints of one composer toward the same poem. A composer's viewpoint is right if it works, re-gardless of the poet's reaction, for the poet will never feel the song as he felt the poem which inspired the song. Debussy, Fauré, and Hahn all used the same verse of Verlaine, all convincingly, all more or less differ-ently. More or less. "Clair de lune" did suggest a similar built-in musical formula to French composers at the turn of the century.

On the principle that there is no one way to musicalize a poem, I once composed a cycle by selecting eight works by as many Americans and setting each one to music twice, each as differently as possible. The per-forming sequence of the sixteen songs was pyramidal: one through eight, then back from eight to one. Although each poem is repeated, none of the music is; thus the poems supposedly take on new impact during a second hearing, not only by virtue of being sung at a later time but also by being reinvested with another form.

❋   ❋   ❋

It goes without saying that I speak here of poetry as distinct from lyrics. Poetry is self-contained, whereas lyrics are made to be sung and do not necesssarily lead a life of their own. Lyricists are collaborative craftsmen. When "real" poets write with song in mind, they fail as poets because, in "helping" the composer, they overindulge in presumably felicitous vocables which emerge as self-conscious banality. To argue that they *hear* what they write is irrelevant to musicians; we have come a long way since Homer, and poems today are mostly made and absorbed in silence. A poet declaiming his own verse is no more definitive, no more *inevitable*, than some composer's setting of that verse. This applies as much to readings of always-the-same verse against never-the-same jazz backgrounds as it does to the embarrassing solo histrionics of a Dylan Thomas or the sabotagingly dry delivery of an Elizabeth Bishop.

❊   ❊   ❊

Elizabeth Bishop in Brazil and I in France corresponded on such matters. Finally in 1957 I made a setting of her masterpiece, "Visits to St Elizabeth's," published it, recorded it with a mezzo soprano, and sent the disk to Rio where it was awaited with high expectations. The tact of Elizabeth's disappointment was touching. "I wonder why you picked a female voice," she wrote in 1964, "and how it would sound with a male voice." Again, in 1968: "Sometime I'd like to write you one small criticism—not the music, of course, but the manner of singing it." Finally in 1969: "My complaint is that it sounds too hysterical. I hadn't imagined it that way, somehow. Yes, I had thought of a male voice, I suppose —but I don't believe that is what bothers me. It is the fast tempo and the increasing note of hysteria. Because the poem is observation, really, rather than participation . . . something like that. Two friends have said rather the same thing to me. It is awfully well sung, nevertheless. I don't know whether it could just be *slowed* down, or not? Probably not." (Cruelly I'm reminded of Saroyan's poignant remark to Paul Bowles about the latter's music for "My Heart's in the Highlands." "Couldn't it be played more—well—in *minor?*")

Poets' work ends with their poems. During the concert they can only weep impotently from the wings, especially when the song succeeds. "Visits to St Elizabeth's" in fact succeeds more than many of my pieces, being often sung and loudly applauded, and singers say it "feels good." How answer Miss Bishop when the song imposes its own terms of longevity?

As to the singer's sex she has a point, but a point of taste, not of quality. In principle, we cannot distinguish blindfolded between male and female pianists, say, or violinists. Thus a composer has a stricter concept of piano and violin attributes than of the human voice. He is more lenient of *varieties* of interpretation given one song by many singers, for a soprano is by definition more "limber" than a baritone. Nothing precludes a woman's persuasively singing a man's song at a faster speed if within the speed she maintains a logical attitude. (The reverse is less convincing, at least in opera, not for musical but for esthetic reasons. Although we may empathize and even weep with Octavian or Cherubino,

a man in a woman's role is only good for a laugh.) As for a man performing the Bishop work, I like the idea, although, since it's a patter song,
the reality would sound top-heavy.

❋   ❋   ❋

Once I judged a contest for young composers. My duty was to select
the best from some two hundred manuscripts. An unconscionable per-
centage were settings of "The Hollow Men," all for male chorus, and all
starting with the first-thing-that-comes-to-mind solution: open parallel
fifths. Which may explain why T. S. Eliot never granted musical rights
to anyone.

❋   ❋   ❋

Not that Howard Moss disapproved of my musicalization of his long
King Midas suite (1961), though certainly his sonorous concept (a concept after the fact) was not like mine. The songs are lean and Western,
whereas he saw (saw, not heard) Eastern opulence. Yet for the final
publication his only request is sizable billing, he being (rightly) more
concerned with publicity than with sabotage. After all, the poetry has not
been stolen: it's still right there in his book.

Poet's names are seldom seen on song covers and usually omitted
from printed song programs. Yet where would the song be without them?
Where, though, would the singer be without the song—the composer
of which is given a proportionately shorter shrift? And returning full
circle, where is the poet without the singer? "But I am not without the
singer," answers the poet. "The singer is myself, and what you call
illuminations are to me evasions."

❋   ❋   ❋

Good poetry does not always lend itself to music; that is, it will not
of itself make good music even if the composer is good. Some poems more
than others cry out to be sung (their author's wishes, like Eliot's, not-
withstanding), though different cries are heeded by different composers
with different viewpoints on dealing with those cries—whether to clarify,
dominate, obscure, or ride on them.

Still, better good poetry than bad. Music, being more immediately
powerful, does tend to invisibilize all poems except bad ones. Despite
popular notions to the contrary, it is a demonstrable fallacy that second-
rate poems make the best songs.

Theodore Chanler may well have become America's greatest composer of the genre had not his small catalog adhered mainly to one poet-aster whose words sound even sillier when they are framed by gorgeous tunes, which, through some inverted irony, end up being subdued by those words. Duparc gained Parnassus on a lifetime output of only thirteen songs; yet I wonder how they would come off with verse other than Baudelaire's. Chanler just may make it on his eight delicious little epitaphs of Walter de la Mare.

❋   ❋   ❋

Despite whatever reputation I may hold in that area, I am not *just* a song composer in the sense that Duparc was. My four-hundred-plus songs written since childhood add up to as many hours' work and as many minutes' hearing, nothing compared to the long labors of my symphonic orchestrations and other large-scale works. Yet because all real music is essentially a vocal utterance, be it "Oh Susannah" or *Le Sacre du Printemps*, I *am* just a song composer.

Less is more, and one great song is worth ten merely adroit symphonies. To say you can have it for a song, is to sell the form cheap.

The form, of course, is whatever the verse dictates. (The verse, so to speak, dictates its own execution order.) Until the age of twenty-three I built my songs largely upon the dictates of "singable" poetry from Sappho through Shakespeare to Hopkins. Then during a decade in Europe I often composed in whatever language I thought I was thinking in. (Incidentally, my songs in French never get done, nor do any French songs by Americans. If a French singer condescends to sing an American song, he—or rather, she: it's invaribly a she—will go all out and learn one in English, *tant bien que mal*. And when an American singer decides to learn a French song, she finds it more *legitimate* to learn one by a Frenchman. Britten has set, in the author's tongue, poems of Holderlin, Rimbaud, even Pushkin, but they are sung mostly by Peter Pears. Nor am I aware that Italians, for instance, are given to performing Britten's marvelous Michelangelo sonnets. Of course, Italians only sing arias anyway.)

During those first twenty years of song writing, I also used regularly (and for the past ten have used only) the sounds I most normally inhale: American poetry, especially that of friends, some of whom made words expressly for my setting. Words, not lyrics.

Take for instance Paul Goodman, who was once my Manhattan

Goethe: the poet to whom I as a balladeer most often returned. From 1946 his verse, prose, and theater beautifully served my short tunes, choruses, and opera. Lives shift, ever faster. We seldom meet anymore, in either speech or song. Paul today seems more drawn toward wisely guiding the political acts of men; this can't be done through poetry. And I grow more withdrawn. Yet lately while rehearsing his songs, all written in France during the early fifties (a period of weep and the world weeps with you), I was rekindled with a need for the words and music of that easier decade. The rekindling has not fired more songs of the same kind, but it has cast light again on a bit of conversation between old friends.

Or take Frank O'Hara, whose early and recent death placed both a shroud and halo over that vital group called The New York School of Poets. The last of several occasions for which we conjointly conceived an idea was a Poulenc memorial. Alice Esty invited this collaboration. Frank made a poem I could not understand and did not want to set. So he made another which I could not understand but wanted to set, and did. As a musician I "understand" poetry not during but only after the fact of setting.

❋   ❋   ❋

Nor do poets *understand* music, thank God. So-called "advanced poets," like O'Hara and Goodman, are usually conservative in their musical taste. How often we find sprinkled through their pages the names of Beethoven, Saint-Saens, Rachmaninoff. A modern artist nourishes at least one conventional hankering; if he has two sisters, one is old and the other young. Within himself are contained mixed media as inherently uneven and differentiated as the now-stylish mixture of mediums outside himself. Frank praises Willem de Kooning while Paul excels in city planning; Lukas Foss talks of Buckminster ("Bucky") Fuller but has never heard of Paul Goodman. And much dance today seems less deranged than the music that supposedly impels it. Music and dance may swing hand in hand but never marry, for if music does impel dance, does dance impel music?

Take also the poet John Ashbery, who writes his "Glazunoviana" (as over in Paris the up-to-date Françoise Sagan drops the name of Brahms!) while editing *Art News* which is, by definition, news. Ashbery provided the words to my vocal trio, "Some Trees" (1968). The words were no problem, for the music does not make them a problem. Were any one to find too great a space between the verse and my notes, it would not, I think, be the poets. Poets want their words (if not their meanings) comprehended. The farther out the poet, the nearer in must be his musician.

❋   ❋   ❋

Because conservative poets feel the same way about their words, but because experimental composers are seldom drawn to these poets, yet because audiences have a hard enough time just "getting" the words of even a MacDowell song, we conclude that all music dealing with words must, to communicate (in the broadest sense), necessarily be simple.

❋   ❋   ❋

I compose what I need to hear because nobody else is doing it.

I represent my times if for no other reason than that I inhabit them. Yet I feel guilty about what I do best—setting words to music. Because it comes easily, meaning naturally, I feel I'm cheating.

❋   ❋   ❋

My songs are love letters. To whom? Like Nabokov, I write "for myself in multiplicate," meaning for friends, those personal extremities. Are unheard melodies sweeter? Intelligence is silence, truth being invisible. But music does not (should not) appeal to our intelligence, nor is it especially concerned with truth any more than poetry is.

Yet we are all afraid of being misrepresented, as though we do not misrepresent ourselves every minute. A song is but a single facet of oneself, which the listener takes as the whole self.

❋   ❋   ❋

In the foregoing do I contradict myself? Very well than, taking good Walt Whitman's prerogative, I contradict myself. Not that, like him, I am large or contain multitudes; but he taught me not to fear contradictions. The purest demonstration of fearlessness is nudity, whose purest demonstration is song, whose purest demonstration is the poet's eternal Myself.

Postscript in Homage to Whitman:

"I pour the stuff to make sons," he exclaimed. Those sons cover the earth, singing for better or worse through the impulse of their fathers. More than anyone in history save Shakespeare, Whitman has appealed to song composers, whatever their style or nationality, possibly because he spoke as much through his voice as through his pen, contagiously craving immortality. "I spring from the pages into your arms," cries the dead author to his living reader.

The act of reading is no more passive than being a spectator at the theater, despite what today's sponsors of total-audience-participation would have us think. To read is to act; it takes two to make a poem; an attentive reader participates constantly. But with Whitman the participation becomes more than usually evident, more physical. The reason may lie in his emphasis on immediate sensation rather than on philosophic introspection. At least that explains his century-old appeal to musicians and his more recent revival within our collective poetic sensibility, specifically with, say, Allen Ginsberg, and generally with the flower children of Pop culture. That explains also why so many primarily instrumental composers, when they do write an occasional song, set the poems of Whitman to music. (Or should I more properly say, set their music to the poems of Whitman!) Finally it explains why primarily vocal composers started early with Whitman, especially during the 1940s when it seemed urgent to be American at any price, and why so many of their songs sing embarrassingly now like the youthful discretions they are. During that same period but for other reasons (reasons of gratitude), certain riper Europeans used Whitman, and used him more touchingly than many of us— Kurt Weill, for example, or Hindemith, whose "When Lilacs Last in the Dooryard Bloom'd" is surely his choral masterwork.

My own choices of words have usually been somehow more practical. When planning to write a song I seek poems more for sound than meaning, more for shape than sentiment. Sometimes (this is a confession), the music being already within me, I will literally take any verse at hand and force it into the preconceived melodic mold. When the outcome "works," it's precisely because I have not wallowed in the sense of the words so much as tried to objectify or illustrate them.

But Whitman has proved exceptional to this kind of choice. For if I loved form for its own sake and challenge, I also loved and needed Whitman, whose style, in a sense, is lack of style, an unprecedented freedom which, with its built-in void of formal versified variety, offers unlimited potential for formal musical variety. Whitman is content. A poet's content is a musician's form; any other way a song is merely redundant and becomes, in the words of Valéry, a painting seen through a stained glass window. Looking back, I find that the dozen Whitman

poems I have musicalized over the years were selected less from intellectual motives than because they spoke to my condition at a certain time. I
adopted them through that dangerous impulse called inspiration, not for
their music but for their meaning.

The first was "Reconciliation," an appeal to my pacifism in time
of war. A few years later "Sometimes with One I Love" so sharply
described my frame of mind that the music served as a sort of superfluous
necessity. But once, when commissioned to provide accompaniments for
recitations of Whitman, I of course failed; for if the human voice in
song is the most satisfying of all instruments—indeed, the instrument all
others would emulate—the spoken voice is the least musical, and a sonic
background to it simply interferes.

Another time, however, I was so overcome by the sensuality of "The
Dalliance of the Eagles" that song was not enough. In a tone poem called
"Eagles" for huge orchestra I composed a purely instrumental tissue on
Whitman's strophic format, and followed (symbolically, if you will) his
development of idea. Listeners, aware of the program, are appropriately
titillated by the sound picture of aereal carnality, though of course no
nonvocal music really connotes an unvariable picture beyond what the
composer tells you, in words, it is supposed to connote.

Contrary in resources, if not in intent, were my settings of five Whitman poems for baritone and clavichord in 1957. And in 1966 I turned
to this catholic writer for help in still another domain. I was plotting a
large-scale suite for voice and orchestra titled *Sun*, and I proposed to use
descriptions of that star by eight poets—from King Ikhnaton in 1360 B.C.
to the late Theodore Roethke. At a loss for a penultimate selection (I
required something tranquil, almost motionless, before the final explo-
sion) I turned to Whitman as naturally as some turn to the Bible and
found, not to my surprise, in his *Specimen Days* a prose paragraph answering my prayers the low key of which proved the high point of the
cycle. He poured the stuff to make *my* sun!

Much current enthusiasm for Whitman, indeed for any admired
artist, centers less in quality per se than in how that quality applies to
our times. We hear a good deal about protest and involvement, with
implicit hints that a committed artist is a good artist—or vice versa. The
premise is false, for talent is conspicuously rarer than integrity. An artist
speaking politics succeeds on the strength of his name, and he is not
speaking art. The prime movers of public thought have never been major
artists, who, almost by definition, are not in positions of authority; when

they are, their art atrophies. Romantic though it sounds, artists need time, time for the introspection of creation. That time cannot be spent in the obligatory extroversion of "committed" oratory. Anyone can be right; nor are artists necessarily invested with rightness. Their function is not to convert so much as to explain pleasurably—albeit with sometimes agonizing pleasure. At least that is how I understand *my* function.

Yet when I consider my musical use of Whitman, I can, in a sense, see it as *engaged*. Still, the song "Reconciliation" is not the product of a pacifist but of a composer who happens to be a pacifist, just as "Sometimes with One I Love" is not the product of a lover but of a composer who once felt the experience. How easy to misread the intent of these songs because they have words! The misreading may declare them good when, in fact, they can be bad. Actually no nonvocal music can be proved to be political or committed, and by extension neither can vocal music nor any other so-called representational art.

Having heart and head well placed, then, does not inherently produce art, though it is safe to assume that most artists are not fools; genius bigots like Wagner are really exceptional. Artistic natures do tend to the left.

Thus it was not Whitman's good intentions that made him what he was, but his expression of those intentions. And with mere contradictory words, what more can I say of Whitman's intentions that, hopefully, I have not said better with notes?

Figure 1

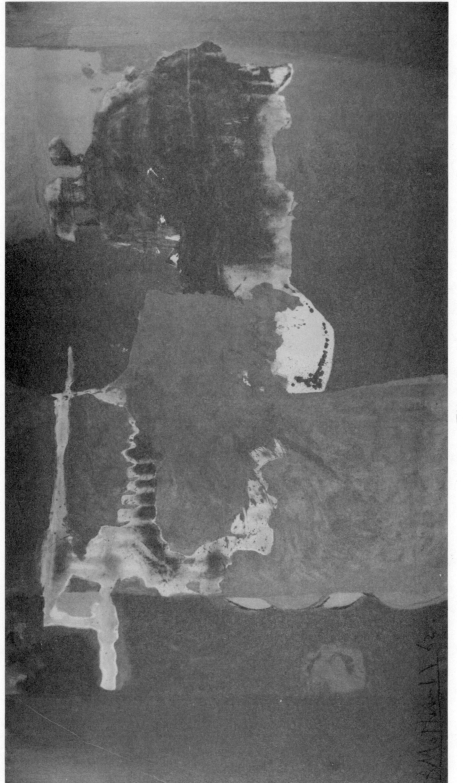

Figure 2

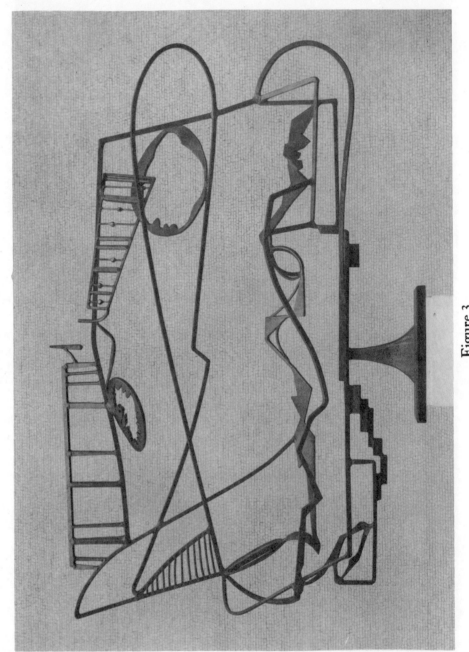

Figure 3

Figure 4

Figure 5

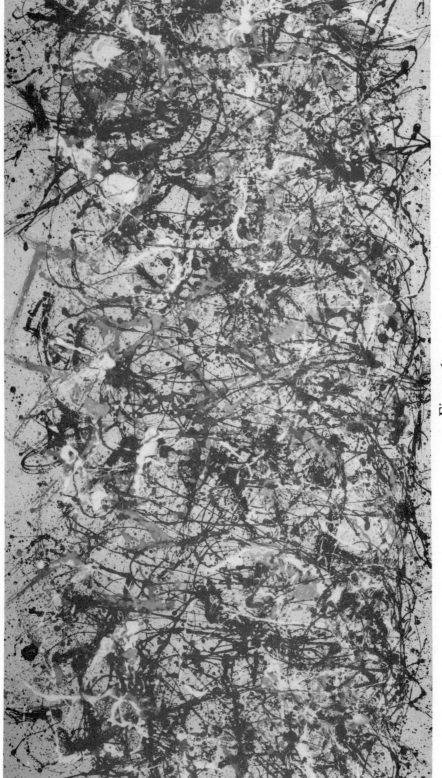

Figure 6

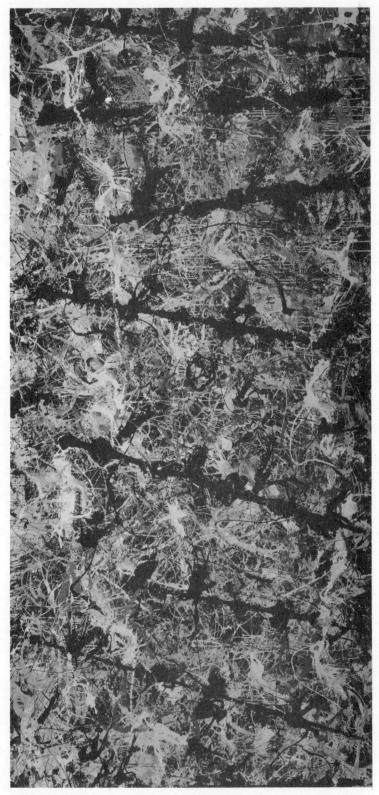

Figure 7

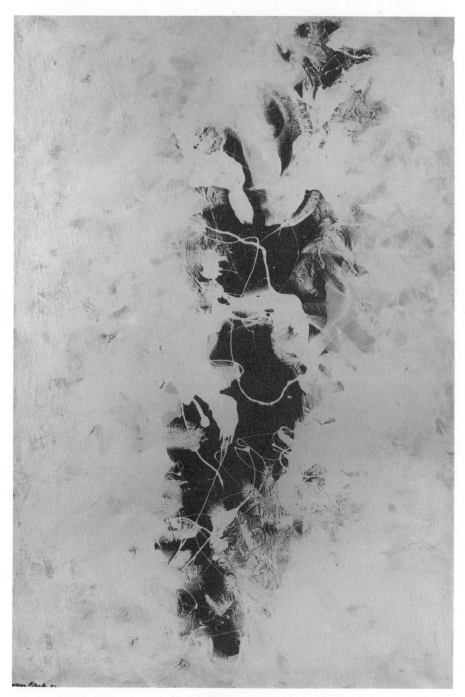

Figure 8

Max Kozloff

Walt Whitman
and American Art

"There is something princely about even the most democratic artists." Few epigrams more clearly characterize than this by Robert Motherwell the visual executors of the estate of Walt Whitman. That they are in many instances unconscious or indirect agents of his patrimony does not diminish their Whitmanesque lineage, for he has complexly suffused American culture for more than a century. From the viewpoint of imagery, there is practically nothing, of course, that is *not* in him, so that talk of his influence upon things visualized in arts other than poetry is completely open-ended, but also in itself unfocused, nonsignificant. However, he shock-welded an autocratic imagination and an egalitarian social conscience in such poetic competition with each other that the end product has persisted incisively ever since in more thwarted, unrelaxed, and combustible styles. It is this competition, being changed through the doubts and grandiosities of American artists, that I propose to examine. Indeed, so resonant has been this "psychic ruckus" exemplified by Whitman, that much of our art appears to be, by and large, a dilation of its central themes.

Gleaned from verbal statements by artists on their own positions (but by no means absent from what they have created), a list of such themes can be enumerated:

the quest for some naked, unequivocal internal identity;

the need to overcome, either by compensation or exaltation, a feeling of solitude;

a nostalgia for some future harmony of understanding in which the individual creator is accepted by the mass of his compatriots as a peer;

anxiety and insecurity about the function of art in a democratic society;

metaphoric overextensions of potency and will, caprice and style, as a means of self-assertion;

mistrust of collective structures and intellectual traditions as enemies of impulse;

macaronic confusions between "high" and "low" art;

mixed sensations of urban and rural experience and messianic aspirations toward a "public" statement; [1]

finally, and conversely, a dedication to artistic effort as labor in which the artist views himself as a blue-collar worker.

Perhaps few of these themes in themselves can be considered exclusive to American art. But if to this mix we add a restless, protean urge to move unhampered by a commitment to the past, if, too, we perceive in all these disturbances, overt or not, a fearful innocence, a large absence of irony, then here, recognizably, are the major stereotypes of the American artist. Obviously, distinctions exist between his view of himself, his attitude toward his art, and meanings inherent in the work. However, it was Whitman, preeminently, magisterially, who advertised the collapse of such distinctions; Whitman, following his bardic demiurge, who hammered out incessantly that pungent megalomania whose anatomy I have just sketched, and whose influence tends to get rediscovered in every generation of our artists. (Nor is this any the less chastened by his statement: "I charge you forever reject those who would expound me for I cannot expound myself. I charge that there be no theory or school founded out of me.")

No one who knows American painters and sculptors, or who has studied the history of their work, is unfamiliar with what eventually has to be labeled the contradictions of the Whitman syndrome. Few writers, however, have brought together the remarkable and endless parallels between word and image, but rather between metaphors, ethics, and formal strategies. Nevertheless, the more evident, if superficial connections, should not be overlooked.

We can find many instances in which Whitman has used subject

1. Appropos of this, Richard Chase, with special reference to Whitman, speaks of "the peculiar pressure a democracy puts on its great writers to become self-publicists, pundits, prophets, theologians. and political oracles."

matter similar to that used by other American artists. That is, we can find various tableaux sometimes greatly removed in time and space from his work, which yet seem to bear a strong relation to some accented feature within it.

Edward Hicks' scenes of beastly and natural paradise, "The Peaceable Kingdom," while far homier, render some of Whitman's harmonious congregations of fauna and flora.

Thomas Cole's "The Titan's Goblet," though its metaphor is naive and literal, depicts a tree, that is, an organic growth, turned into a vessel containing whole worlds from which the poet himself appears to drink throughout his vision (though Cole derived his subject from the Norse legend of The Tree of Life).

And what of Erastus Salisbury Field's "Historical Monument of the American Republic," of 1876, which appropriately visualizes Whitman's lines: "And thou, high-towering One—America! Thy swarm of offspring towering high—yet higher thee, above all towering. With Victory on thy left, and at thy right Law; Through Union, holding all-fusing, absorbing, tolerating all . . . ?"

The coincidence of the primitive imagination, Hicks' allusion to the eleventh chapter of Isaiah, the dream of the triumphant Republic envisaged in a babel of Biblical towers, of the natural concourse and fusion of past and future—all this is unmistakably linked with the central thrust of Whitman's poetics. For *Leaves of Grass* is like a cosmological sieve, through which beautiful animal scurryings testify to the creative faculties of man that transcend time and history, yet, paradoxically, marry him to the soil and the polis. In their fabulous, archaic, and above all allegorical, fashion, these paintings allude to that benevolent licentiousness, or omniscient embrace, confessing itself alien to nothing, which is the lodestar of Whitman's program.

The poet's own taste in art disowns anything so childlike and romantic as the paintings I've just mentioned. Not that there aren't callow stretches or romantic clichés in Whitman's thinking, but they do not zero in on that particular enchantment which was readily materialized in certain pictorial and poetic conventions. Hardly any consciously poetic, that is, refined, American painting has much to do with Whitman's verse. On the contrary, as a critic of the Brooklyn Art Union show of 1851, he plumped for a visual art that would be socially engagé—"ardent, radical, and progressive" are his words—in short, he aspired to see some equivalent of those realist currents that were then eagerly espoused by the humanitarian critics of Paris. Perhaps no poet misrepresented himself or another artist in such large measure as the Whitman who could say, "The *Leaves* are really only Millet in another form." If the ethic of Barbizon was a popular taste brought back to the States by William Morris Hunt, most prominently, Whitman, more than others, seems to have found in it a correspondence with his own radical, if not revolutionary, outlook.

Whitman was as incapable of the sentimentalism of Millet—if only to preserve many options for himself—as he was free from the chronic habit of making idealistic generalizations from particular observations. Possibly the element that appealed to him most in Millet, aside from the painter's obvious empathy with the life of common people, was the song, or chantlike sensibility, of the French master—though probably the euphony of light rather than of mild painterly rhythms provided the object of admiration. Even so, the artistic diffidence of Barbizon could not have been congenial for a man to whom all perception, as indeed all poetic art, was a function of his own re-creating self. For Whitman, perception, far more than concept or transcript, was a concrete thing. The only nineteenth-century painter who offered a parallel—and here a very close one—to Whitman's temperamental approach and life style, was Courbet. How illustrative of Courbet's key work, "L'Atelier," are Whitman's words: "I am personal. . . . In my poems, all revolves round, concentrates in, radiates from myself. I have but one central figure, the general human personality typified in myself." The brawny rustic, the self-made man who considers all experience *lebensraum* for his perpetually extending, magniloquent, but sense-rooted art, is a type exceptional in European culture; he was not to appear among American painters until well into the twentieth century.

Yet this personality, as incarnated in Whitman, modulates into some haunting, if well-known, contradictions. The more he presumes to speak for other men, for instance—the more encompassing his vision—the less he can lay claim to originality, the less he can be said to have any individual voice at all. Borges speaks of the Whitman who, "with *impetuous humility*, yearns to be like all men" [italics mine]. Because the sage from Paumanok was no more like other men than the experimental *Leaves of Grass* was like other poetry, this yearning to submerge himself into the cultural horizon exposed an intolerable consciousness of his apartness, something that had to be mended at whatever (self-defeating) cost to coherence and whatever sacrifice of a plausible narrative identity. Thus the otherworldliness that causes one to blink at such lines as, "These are really the thoughts of all men in all ages and lands, they are not original with me." And if this is followed by the highly moralistic communion of, "If they are not yours as much as mine they are nothing, or next to nothing" ["Song of Myself," Section 17], it only indicates the will to achieve some fictional fusion of author and reader, in flesh as well as mind, that could only be realized in language that has no one location or vantage, language that issues from a body that has no one sex, up- bringing, or age. That is why, although Whitman always announces he is at ease with nature, he appears not to be of it, and it illuminates the incipient symbolism that overcasts his realism—something so wonderfully strange as a great carnal appetite invoked at a seance. No wonder Borges was moved at the spectacle of a poetic corpus that vacuums away its author's earthly existence into multiple *personae* conversing with them- selves, generating everywhere and nowhere—and that yet acknowledges its own contradictions.

The pantheism that inflected Whitman makes it difficult to arrive at some conclusion about his aesthetic inclinations. Evidence is available that he took a confusedly idealistic-pragmatic view of optical sensation, warn- ing himself to avoid making his poems "in the spirit that comes from the study of pictures of things—and not from the spirit that comes from the real things themselves." His cult of immediacy, however, did not preclude a great sympathy with such Swedenborgian strictures of George Inness as, "Art is the endeavor on the part of the mind to express through the senses, ideas of the great principles of unity." Whitman is hostile to visual, if not poetic, metaphor because it is a species of allusion, whereas, what is wanted, somehow, is the presence of the thing itself; yet "word-things" must still correspond to "ideas." He is ambivalent, finally, about realism because its imitative transparency seems to him to operate outside expres- sive language, even as it vitally transcribes experience. The Whitmanesque lists, therefore, are as much abstractions as they are observations, frozen sightings in the form of static litany. His critics have put it very well. R. W. B. Lewis says, "The things that are named seem to spring into being at the sound of the word." Charles Feidelson, Jr., states that "the antirationalism of the romantic voyage is a wilful projection of feeling; the romantic sea is the image of a world subservient to emotion. But the symbolistic voyage is a process of becoming: Whitman is less concerned with exploration of emotion than with exploration as a mode of existence. Similarly, his poems not only are *about* voyaging, but also *enact* the voyage." [2]

No painter of his time would seem to be more at odds with this enactment, and yet none was held in greater esteem by Whitman, than Thomas Eakins. Eakins' highly structured laboriousness, his obsession with science, and his illusionism would appear to make his position antithetical to that of the "good gray poet." However, Whitman's only fears, unjustified as it turned out, were that the portrait that Eakins painted would be too glum. The image that the most penetrating American portraitist of the age gives of its greatest poet, however, strikes us as nuanced with mobile and benevolent ambiguity. [See plate 26.] A coarse, ruddy, and wrinkled old face, half veiled in shadow and smogged by beard, a hooded twinkle of the eyes, untidy, but with clean, lace-fringed collar, the body thrust up close to the picture plane, diagonally athwart the glance. It is a compelling mixture of assertion and passivity. Of this subtle perpetuation of his own myth, Whitman, at first doubtful, warmed with praise: "Tom's portraits . . . are not a remaking of life, but life, its manifests, just as it is, as they are." It is no more literally true than his remark: "I never knew of but one artist, and that's Tom Eakins, who could resist the temptation to see what they thought ought to be rather than what is." But at another point, Whitman can say, "We need a Millet in portraiture—a man who sees the spirit but does not make too much of it—one who sees the flesh but does not make a man all flesh—all of him body." Eakins "almost achieves this balance—almost—not quite: Eakins errs just a little —a little—in the direction of the flesh." [3] To hear the poet retract somewhat about the equilibrium of Eakins' work is not, however, to diminish the respect for him as a "force"—particularly in the apparently unvarnished, unconventional presence of Eakins' realization of the image in paint—his strenuous honesty and his lack of artiness.

Eakins, far from being a rebel (except insofar as his professional hardheadedness clashed with genteel society) was one of those homegrown individualists for whom nature, far more than tradition, is the guidepost of artistic labor. "The big artist," he wrote his father, "does not sit down

2. R. W. B. Lewis, *The American Adam* (Chicago: The University of Chicago Press, 1955), p. 51; Charles Feidelson, Jr., *Symbolism and American Literature* (Chicago: The University of Chicago Press, 1953), pp. 26–27 [my italics].

3. Quoted by F. O. Matthiessen, *American Renaissance: Art and Expression in the Age of Emerson and Whitman* (New York: Oxford University Press, 1941), p. 604.

monkey-like and copy a coal-scuttle or an ugly old woman like some Dutch painters have done, nor a dung pile, but he keeps a sharp eye on Nature and steals her tools. He learns what she does with light, the big tool, and then color, then form, and appropriates them to his own use. Then he's got a canoe of his own, smaller than Nature's, but big enough for every purpose. . . . With this canoe he can sail parallel to Nature's sailing." [4] The egotistical modesty which deems him capable of finding a parallel to nature (actually an aspiration going back to the Renaissance), the Whitmanesque sense of being on a frontier, taking a voyage, and the vessel of transport itself, a canoe, than which nothing could be more American—all this makes for a priceless statement. Important to notice here is the implication that the artistic enterprise is hardly what one may call spontaneous. Not only are there many false leads in voyages through time and space, but the sense of the unknown forces as much prior mapping of the terrain as possible in Eakins and endless revision in the more expansive Whitman. (Much the same applies to Inness, for whom the act of painting constituted immense torture, freshness itself lost and regained, hated and adored.) Eakins, who admired the work of his sitter no less than that of his other favorite author, Rabelais, thought that "Whitman never made a mistake." He can be right in the sense that there could be no mistake only because there could not be, aesthetically, a destination —no end to the open road.

With the advent of the twentieth century, and its retreat from likeness, the issues of realist doctrine dissolve, but problems of symbolism and the anxiety of the artist over his role increase radically. The artist no longer feels that he can give naturally of himself and pertain to outer, observed nature. He must assume some mage-like importance, an elitist purpose that synthesizes experience on a level that may be coded, but demands the participative spectator. Or he reverts to the pretended status of an artisan in order to establish kinship with that spectator. In this difficult relationship with himself and his audience, heightened after the Armory Show of 1913 by the knowledge of how much he had to catch up with his European colleagues, the "Whitmanesque syndrome" surfaces within the personality of the American artist as it never had before.

Perhaps John Marin will stand as one example which reflects the equivocal traits that lead back vividly to Whitman. Marin was a flinty, folksy character, probably the latest among the serious artists of this century, to use the verbal slang of the last, who struggles with himself

4. Quoted by Matthiessen, p. 606.

under the burden of a spiritualism that wants, as it were, to *naturalize* creativity itself. What forms under his brush is a source of naive wonder. Speaking of his abstracting of a ship's prow, one of his recurring themes, he writes: "Mr. Fisherman, he doesn't maybe understand, yet he's made to feel something like he feels as he knows prows of ships." Or the touching confusion of the following: "If I put down things haphazard, without meaning to myself, I'd say good, I am crazy and let it go at that. But this seemingly crazy stroke is put down with deliberate, mulish wilfulness. And when I get through they look so much like Marin, they act like Marin. Cannot I ever get away from this fellow Marin?" How curiously this recalls that line from "Song Of Myself": "I believe in you my soul, the other I am must not abase itself to you."

Marin exacerbates himself with his own dividedness: "There are moments when I am unbelievably in love with myself. But, there are moments when I unbelievably hate myself. . . . Hating everything foreign, to a degree, with the opposite coming, time and time. A shouting spread-eagled American, a drooping wet winged sort of nameless fowl the next." These may be considered the characteristic hesitations of a high-strung artist whose style, in its borrowed cubist planes that jangle against his more phenomenal yet symbolistic shorthand for weather and energy, often betrays unresolved tensions or flounders in stereotypes. Marin, however, takes a most evident refuge from his doubts in a pose that strikes us as Whitmanesque: "Yes I'll have it that painting is a *Job*—a *Job* in paint—and I'm afraid that in the crazed desire to be modern—to have ideas—to be original—to belong to the tribe *intelligence*—we have gotten away from the paint job which is a *lusty thing* . . . at the present I sing to the *Lusty*." It is quite clear from this statement, not only that Marin wants to equate art with a kind of job, the activity of its potent, life-celebrating, to be sure, but also that his equation masks an attempted escape from the modern and from the responsibility to develop ideas.

Discords such as these are engulfed by the rhetoric of the abstract expressionists during the forties, in which the embattled artist valorizes his calling in tones of almost Promethean belligerence. Nowhere previously in American art (with an exception in architecture to which I will come shortly) is there such a consistent, straining will to painterly power, such a protestation of masculinity, materializing, however, in an aesthetic of risk and self-chastisement that almost caricatures its deep affinity with the Whitman legend. Significantly, for the first time, there had evolved a pictorial vocabulary, fully confident now of its momentum away from

Europe, which demonstrates innumerable sympathies with the voluble space and cosmic scale of Whitman's poetry. Crucial is the fact that at last painting takes hold of a metaphor in which materialization of form, allusive imagery, and the gesturing of the creative act are condensed into one Adamic presence, a "thing" we might consider like the energetic rebirth of language striven for by Whitman. The abstract-expressionist painting, moreover, is stressed in terms of an exploration, or rather derives its content—emotional and symbolic—from the circular, if exalted, reference to what it is apparently doing: voyaging. And lastly, the overall figuration of this painting, its ontological phrasing, as it were, is ejaculatory. Think of how physically emblematic is this art of Whitman's sentence: "I effuse my flesh in eddies, and drift it in lacy jags" ["Song of Myself," Section 52].

Recent studies have sketched some of the pictorial and iconographical affinities abstract-expressionist painting has with traditions of Northern romantic landscape art and eighteenth-century concepts of the Sublime (the latter a contentious subject among the painters themselves). Thanks to current scholarship, we know a great deal about the surrealist legacy of automatism as it variously affected certain members of the New York School. If in the claims they make for themselves, that is, the psychology which made their art possible, did not also justify it (and there is much evidence that they wanted it to), we find a spirit no less transcendental than Whitman. "O," sings the poet, "the joy of my soul leaning pois'd on itself, receiving identity through materials and loving them, observing characters and absorbing them. . . . The real life of my senses and flesh transcending my senses and flesh. . . . To be indeed a God!" ["A Song of Joys"].

Listen to Barnett Newman: "Instead of making *cathedrals* out of Christ, man, or 'life' we are making [art] out of ourselves, out of our own feelings. The image we produce is the self-evident one of revelation, real and concrete, that can be understood by anyone who will look at it without the nostalgic glasses of history." [5] [See plate 1.] Or listen to Adolph Gottlieb:

---

5. With a feeling of considerable pride, Newman once reminded me of a poem written about his work by Howard Nemerov, in 1958:

On Certain Wits
who amused themselves over the simplicity of Barnett Newman's paintings shown at Bennington College in May 1 of 1958

"When I say I am reaching for a totality of vision I mean that I take the things I know—hand, nose, arm—and use them in my paintings after separating them from their associations as anatomy. . . . It's a primitive method, and a primitive method of expressing without learning how to do so by conventional ways. . . . It puts us at the beginning of seeing." Of his work Clyfford Still observes: "There I had made it clear that a single stroke of paint, backed by work and a mind that understood its potency and implications, could restore to man the freedom lost in twenty centuries of apology and devices for subjugation." Perfectly in accord are Robert Motherwell's sentiments expressed to me in an interview: "Perhaps, someday, when we no longer threaten our contemporaries, someone will write our *Iliad* with empathy. One of the great images, like Achilles' shield, should be the housepainter's brush, in the employ of a grand vision, dominated by an ethical sensibility that makes the usual painter's brush indeed picayune." [See plate 2.] Nor could there be anything more summary of the Olympian strain in this aesthetic than David Smith's pronouncement: "I feel no tradition. I feel great spaces. I feel my own time. I am disconnected. I belong to no mores—no party—no religion —no school of thought—no institution. I feel raw freedom and my own identity." [6] [See plate 3.] Jackson Pollock, perhaps, puts it even more simply: when told by Hans Hofmann that he should work after nature, he expostulated, "I am nature." [See plates 5-8.] Similarly, Whitman begins a poem: "Spontaneous me, nature."

It would be as thankless to separate existentialism from chiliasm in

---

> When Moses in Horeb struck the rock,
> And water came forth out of the rock,
> Some of the people were annoyed with Moses
> And said he should have used a fancier stick.
>
> And when Elijah on Mount Carmel brought the rain,
> Where the prophets of Bael could not bring rain,
> Some of the people said that the rituals of the
>   prophets of Bael
> Were aesthetically significant, while Elijah's
>   were very plain.

6. Smith, in another mood, was more undecided: "By choice I identify myself with workingmen and still belong to Local 2054 United Steelworkers of America. I belong by craft—yet my subject of aesthetics introduces a breach. I suppose that it is because I believe in a workingman's society in the future and in that society I hope to find a place. In this society I find little place to identify myself economically." Cleve Gray, ed., *David Smith by David Smith* (New York: Holt, Rinehart and Winston, 1968), p. 61.

these postures as it would be idle to speculate on the degree of credence to attach to them. From today's vantage, such swami talk was an authentic means of letting off steam, the confirmation of certain imperatives in their art. To sire the never-before, to metamorphosize knowledge into commanding innocence, to fling a gauntlet at the past and the public: these challenges are manifested earlier in modern painting, but never so self-reflexively raging to be free, unburdened of contingency, and, above all, of bodily repression. That this stance comes charged, paradoxically, with the most high-minded moralism reveals its cross purposes, too, for the resources and energies of the artists are pressurized by the responsibility to make every stroke a meaningful confession—in situations that cannot be foreseen—situations represented by the canvases of the future. A remarkable blend of idealism and pragmatism results. Harold Rosenberg makes a parable of it by his term "Coonskinism," defined as "the search for the principle that applies, even if it applies only once. For it, each situation has its own exclusive key. Hence general knowledge of his art does not abate the Coonskinner's ignorance nor relieve him of the need to improvise. . . . Out of the Bible, Homer, the newspapers, opera, Whitman puts together poetry from which the appearance of poetry has managed to depart." The context of these remarks seeks to describe the origins of the ad-libbing "non-look" in American art in those sets of given stylistic options from which our most original artists flee toward urgent, makeshift, composite strategies that crystallize certain psychic responses long before they are accepted as "art." Conscious of their own hit-and-miss process, and vulnerable to it, abstract expressionists, almost in self-defense, formulate their mythic humanism, absolutize their transient sense of victory. It may not be in Walt Whitman exclusively, but in him predominantly this American creative mentality established itself.

Apart from the polemical liaison painting of the New York School at times shows startling correspondence to the poetic subjects and forms of *Leaves of Grass*. Both sing "the body electric" in their rippling patterns of material that personifiy nature as a muscular system braided with intelligent fibers, grafting to, and yet cleaving from, the ground. The mind often has to flag down Whitman's images and thoughts, for even his titles prepositionally sprint into meaning. So too does the brush of De Kooning, gliding over the surface on the upswing. Moreover, the tactility evoked in the poems—liquid, rugged, adhesive, dense—has a somatic life which finds its counterpart in the painting, rife also with allusion to visceral activity. There is a glandular alertness in both arts. The frequent mixed use of the imperative and exclamatory, the oracular and the colloquial, is also shared by the poetry and the painting. The endless, glutted, plasmic spreads of the Whitman song, often without marked beginning or end, subordinate or dominant theme, show forth that atomized, attention-diffusing "all-overness" embodied in the work of Pollock (not to speak of the unselfconscious willingness to incorporate accidents, enhanced seismograph of the personal). The space of Whitman contrives to juxtapose the intimately seen and immensely far in an ambiguous narrative that parallels the shifting accommodation the eye makes to the metaphorical depths of action painting. The mind encounters no resistance as it moves from the tiny to the grandiose in these arts, although the jostling of their elements is pervaded by unacknowledged physical discontinuities.[7] Finally, just as Whitman's art is more tonal than chromatic, with intimations and fragments of modeling strewn throughout, so too is the work of the abstract expressionists, with the exception of color-field painting.

American art of the late fifties and sixties, though it maintains innovation and quality, witnesses a collapse of strained heroism and with it much of the Whitman ethos. A kind of laissez faire styling comes to the fore, behind which specialized ironic, or phlegmatic, conceptual assaults work coldly upon the spectator. Above all, the artist distances the personal implications of his work, the "what" of it becoming more important than the camouflaged "who" behind it. It might be said that the happenings movement, in the openness of its performances and its adrenal rummaging

7. Thomas Hess has many interesting things to say about this problem in the art of De Kooning: "One of the decisions many New York artists made in the 1940's was to have their painting mean anything and everything. From this it followed that the studio should be everywhere and anywhere. The painting and the studio, the streets outside, the drive through the country that led away from and back to the easel, all merged into the painting. . . . He [De Kooning] recaptures complex illusions of depth by making the image all of a piece; with no pauses or rests, no in-betweens." *Willem De Kooning* (New York: George Braziller, 1959), p. 19.

For his part, David Smith gives an account of one of his sculptures, "Hudson River Landscape," which "started from drawings made on a train between Albany and Poughkeepsie, a synthesis of drawings from 10 trips going and coming over this 75 mile stretch. On this basis I started a drawing for a sculpture. As I began, I shook a quart bottle of India ink, it flew over my hand, it looked like my landscape. I placed my hand on paper and from the image this left I travelled with the landscape to other landscapes and their objects, with additions, deductions, directives which flashed past too fast to tabulate. . . ." *David Smith by David Smith*, p. 71. [See plate 3.]

of the American place, contains much that relates to our theme. However, the critical Dada prerequisites at its base and the more subtle ethic of programmed chance techniques clash with an older instinctual expressionism. Some of the color painting that comes out of Pollock (the orgiastic Morris Louis, for example) could be included in the Whitman poetic line. For the most part, current abstract painting swerves into the well-known systems and series which graph its reaction to the painterliness of its mentor. In large measure pop art, too, would seem to disqualify itself from a Whitmanesque impulse because of its endorsement of commercial-industrial media for formal purposes far removed from any democratic humanism. Yet, one figure, Claes Oldenburg, does emerge out of pop art to reclaim the Whitman vision with the most implausible, grotesque secularizing splendor. [See plate 4.]

Oldenburg, it seems to me, is unique among the pop artists in realizing, deep in his artistic innards, that commercial pop-kitsch culture constitutes the only real form of folk culture our country has had and that serious art can materialize all its implications. For him, the dream of the American world empire, that dreamy democratic hegemony, fuses the dribblings from the slums and the streets, and more recently, a vision of giant vinyl appliances, tools, and foodstuffs, from whose flatulence air is being let out. Disillusioned and clownish, he has no need to come to skittish terms with the earth, for, all along, the natural pedestal for his sentiments has been the floor. Yet he is the most spectacular exponent of Whitmania—on all fours, groping hilariously, groveling in its own ridiculousness. Here is one coonskinner with comic and carnal knowledge of himself: "My approach is a direct strong vulgarity/Lisztian Beethovian Brueghelian Orozcoan Whitmanian Rabelaisian/including delicacy." [8] Moreover, perception is a matter always of visual, as it frequently is of verbal, puns: "I sing the bawdy electric. I sew the Broadway galactic. I slang the body eclectic." His peculiar irreverence consists of seeing, as Whitman could not literally see, yet in accord with, or parallel to, Whitman's thought, the mutability of all forms and things into each other—existence as a spewing of "impossible" resemblances, art as punning on nature, nature as punning on art. ("Sherwin Williams was right: the world is round and full of paint.")

Indeed, it's fruitful to look upon Oldenburg's art as an extension of

8. Claes Oldenburg, *Store Days* (New York: Something Else Press, Inc., 1967), p. 60.

pantheism strained through the commercial media, and made to giggle.[9] Or rather, as a kind of divine scatology. Yet, nothing if not contradictory, he confesses to didactic aims: "I use naive imitation. This is not because I have no imagination or because I wish to say something about the every-day world. . . . If I alter, which I do usually, I do not alter for 'art' and I do not alter to express *myself*, I alter to unfold the object, and to add to it other object-qualities, forces . . . art can really be useful—by setting an example of how to use the senses." [10] Here one of the great paradoxes emerges in Oldenburg's complete negation of futurity, let alone the utopianism of the transcendentalists, at the same time as the extremes to which the imagination of his own senses propel him lead to a vast spill-over of projects not realizable in the present.

If his vision is ahead of his contemporaries, it is not so because of program, but because of a fantastic inadvertence, a short-term involve-ment with perceptions absurd in proportion to the degree they are inti-mate and familiar. "I am for art that is put on and taken off, like pants, which develops holes, like socks, which is eaten, like a piece of pie, or abandoned with great contempt, like a piece of shit. . . . I am for art that coils and grunts like a wrestler. I am for art that sheds hair. . . . I am for the art of bar-babble, tooth-picking, beerdrinking, egg-salting, in-sult-ing. I am for the art of falling off a barstool." [11] Whole tufts of com-parable body-smelling word-play can be extracted from Whitman, too: "Echoes, ripples, buzz'd whispers, love-root, silk-thread, crotch and vine," or "The scent of these arm-pits aroma finer than prayer." It requires no speculation to see not only the aping of Whitman's sonic sense but also the fundamental participation in the poet's covenant with all that is somatically "ignoble." Oldenburg stands Whitman's lofty concept of art on its head, literalistically (at least on paper) letting all the sweats, excre-ments, and salts of life drool down to displace "art." It represents a vast difference in consciousness. The one sensibility takes Faustian pride in

9. Not that there are no comic patches in Whitman suggestive of the same theme. Take, for instance, that section from "Song of the Exposition" where the muse of poetry is

> Bluff'd not a bit by drain-pipe, gasometers, artificial
>   fertilizers,
> Smiling and pleas'd with palpable intent to stay,
> She's here, install'd among the kitchen ware!

10. Oldenburg, p. 48.
11. *Ibid.*, pp. 39, 41.

its capacity for self-debasement, being, in fact, able to soar ethically above others for that very reason; the other never pretends to any moral footage whatsoever, but quickens in the slime with cruel and ironic jocularity.

About Oldenburg, there is often an outlandish, perplexing diffidence. Calling the bluff of every technological and historical shibboleth, he is still not able to extricate himself from the suffocation of uselessness—while his very clarity makes him less and less philosophically acceptable to himself. Work, and he is one of the most prolific of all contemporary artists, is an insatiable refuge, and more than that, a transparent camouflage: "I have imitated, parodied certain professions—all taken more seriously in the US than the profession of art: f.ex. the house painter, the sign painter, the advertising artist. Also the manufacturer, the merchant, the pastry cook. Now I am beginning to parody the scientist and the inventor. . . . While reading of Edison I am 'inventing' the telephone and so on." The rage to be many personalities, to have many skills, merging with his obsession to make over the world, converts into unease his own playfulness. His desire to imitate and to make connections and have authentic experience can be slated only for charades. Despite all this furious effort, perhaps because of it, Oldenburg's art constantly suggests imminent paralysis and the final seepages of vitality. Rather than budding forth, everything in his vision is coming to rest or falling into a coma. Possibly this makes more understandable his comment (hardly an orthodox point of view for literary critics) that "Whitman is concerned primarily with time. There is about him a time sense which is frightening. He is the master of nothing happening. He is supersensitive to silences and long periods. He is wrapped in time." [12]

There has been a subsequent development of this Rabelaisian pessimism in American art. Its arch representative is the young, Borges-crazed Robert Smithson, whose sculpture is a visual equivalent, or sometimes a mere footnote, to a prose announcement of tired apocalypse. Smithson is "for" an art whose "lethargy is elevated to the most glorious magnitude." He sees in entropy a desirable condition for a minimal sculpture that is involved "in a systematic reduction of time down to fractions of seconds. . . . this kind of time has little or no space; it is stationary and without movement, it is going nowhere. . . . Time becomes a place minus motion." In this aesthetic, immobility is an entrance card into the fourth dimension, a realm conceived and consumed in laughter. Smithson hypothesizes that there are "different types of Generalized Laughter, according to the six

12. *Ibid.*, p. 138.

main crystal systems: the ordinary laugh is cubic or square (Isometric); the chuckle is a triangle or pyramid (Tetragonal); the giggle is a hexagon . . . etc." [13]

Far from fining down possibilities to a state of suspended animation, this Gargantuan stillness is meant to explode limits of consciousness and transform the American landscape into a scene whereby every suggestion of the future is also a reflection of a primordial past. (Had the public quite foreseen, incidentally, that the photos taken from Apollo 8 show us an earth existing in the present, to be sure, but looking also "impossibly" as it was hundreds of thousands of years ago or that, in fact, the light of certain stars now reaching us is millions of years old?) As Oldenburg exfoliates Whitman in terms of pop culture, Smithson, unknowingly, does the same on the level of science fiction. Like Thomas Cole and Erastus Field, Smithson is searching for monuments. Only he is excited by that condition of our environment in which everything seems to be declining into nullity, returning to omniscient insignificance. Speaking of certain contracting sites in Passaic County, New Jersey, he says, "That zero panorama seemed to contain *ruins in reverse*, that is,—all the new construction that would eventually be built. This is the opposite of the 'romantic ruin' because the buildings don't *fall* into ruin *after* they are built but rather *rise* into ruin *before* they are built. . . . His Passaic replaced Rome as The Eternal City?" [14] Smithson anticipates our release from the anchorage of all circumstance and location, not in the burlesque bodily effusions of Oldenburg's "dog turds tall as cathedrals," but as a feature of the abstract reversibility of a discredited linear time, now seen to round, as Borges thought it rounding, on the wheel of a miraculous, but indifferent, reincarnation of spirit. In the context of American art history, we can view this ruins in reverse thesis as emotionally compensatory for certain lacunae in our national experience. As the art critic, Barbara Rose, puts it: "Minimal art responds to an . . . important aspect of the environment: the American landscape, with its anonymous factories and water towers, and its painful absence of classical monuments. Indeed one might see Minimal art as the last act in the drama of the conflict between the American landscape, itself heroic and monumental, and the demands of

13. Robert Smithson, "Entropy and the New Monuments," *Artforum*, IV (June, 1966), 31.
14. Robert Smithson, "The Monuments of Passaic," *Artforum*, VI (December, 1967), 50–51.

the absent monument, the man-made embodiment of these traditional classic ideals." [15]

Smithson has recently descended into his most elevated proclamation on an art that has no choice but to chip at, to erode, and to dig away at the soil itself, an art that he has launched, with others, under the rubric "Earthworks." Excavations, mole-like furrows, liners, sunken sinks, trenches, pee-wee mine shafts, and budget quarrying have been some of the forms taken by this art, spread out obscurely and haphazardly across the continental United States. With a poetic logic as subterranean as his art, Smithson fancies the mind itself a geological phenomenon: "One's mind and the earth are in a constant state of erosion, mental rivers wear away abstract banks, brain waves undermine cliffs of thought, ideas decompose into stones of unknowing. . . ." Or: "Solids are particles built up around flux, they are objective illusions supporting grit, a collection of surfaces ready to be cracked. All chaos is put into the dark inside of the art. By refusing 'technological miracles' the artist begins to know the corroded moments, the carboniferous states of thought, the shrinkage of mental mud. . . . When the fissures between mind and matter multiply into an infinity of gaps, the studio begins to crumble and fall like The House of Usher, so that mind and matter get endlessly confounded." [16]

Such reveries on dissolution suggest a haunting and unwitting precedent in the ecology of Whitman's poetic cosmos. We cannot imagine Whitman writing with an altogether straight face the stupefying line: "I find I incorporate gneiss, coal, long-threaded moss, fruits, grains, esculent roots" ["Song of Myself," Section 31]. It was surely a less comic mood which led him to say, in "A Song of the Rolling Earth:"

> I swear the earth shall surely be complete to him or her who
> shall be complete,
> The earth remains jagged and broken only to him or her who
> remains jagged and broken.
> I swear there is no greatness or power that does not emulate
> those of the earth,

. . . .

15. Barbara Ross, "The Politics of Art, Part II," *Artforum*, VII (January, 1969), 45.

16. Robert Smithson, "A Sedimentation of the Mind," *Artforum*, VII (September, 1968), 49.

I swear I begin to see little or nothing in audible words,
All merges toward the presentation of the unspoken meanings
    of the earth,

. . . .

Toward him who makes the dictionaries of words that print
    cannot touch.

Although both artists agree to lave soil with thought, to blend organic and inorganic, and to find some new articulation stratified in paleolithic matter, the figure of their speech could not be more antithetical. For Whitman, the metaphor is one of blooming, vagrant fertility whose cthonic workings manifest some ultimate Godhead, dissolving into the elements. For Smithson, as in a mirror image or a movie run in reverse, the earth takes back into itself an imagination intoxicated with oblivion. Whitman celebrates growth; Smithson exalts a kind of distracted decay. One mind is "wet," the other is "dry." What is important about the polemical similes of earthworks is that they are grand and as open as the prospecting of Whitman, but they are also its negative. Art is abolished in a calcified firmament of ceaseless, changeful matter.

Leaving aside these Byzantine intrigues with grit, we need to return above ground to see in what manner there has been any attempt to give solid form and social dimension to any of Whitman's theses about democracy. Insofar as the question can even be approached, its answer lies within the medium of architecture.

It must be said at once that architecture as a trade may not in its actual existence and function endorse that forceful impulse *against* authority and doctrine which informs Whitman's scheme of things. At most, architects deal in a constructive, possibly corporate, and nominally accommodating planning of services and shelters, usually abetted by the conservative powers that be. Theirs, after all, is the real world of community and compromise rather than the fantasy or slapstick realm of poets and artists. What made it inevitable that Louis Sullivan and Frank Lloyd Wright should be passionate admirers of Whitman were their profound individuality and their compulsion to "universalize" a new ultra-accessible architecture for the democratic masses. Coming later in our history than Whitman, they were to see enough of philistine materialism to disappoint their hopes for the America of their present; in fact, the tendency of their embittered outlook, actually latent all along, was to make over the inhabitant to the building, or ride roughshod over his character, rather than modulate the building according to the needs of the occupant. In practice, this tension produced a number of aristocratic masterpieces overlaid with an egalitarian symbolism or functionalism. In theory, it emitted logorrheic volumes which attempted to prove the utterly untenable and Whitmanian (as well as Emersonian) exhortation that the inner conviction of the creator subsisted in all men—"mute, inglorious Miltons" who had merely to heed the masterful example of the lone genius to kindle their own potentialities.[17] We are tempted to think that this bogus peerage rested on the guilt of men who upheld architecture as a truly republican force for solidarity, first and most democratic among the arts, and who yet had no choice but to erect monuments to their own ego. Rather than resign themselves to public incomprehension, Sullivan and Wright entertained the flattering delusion that the country could be turned into one vast society of inspired rebels on the basis of the models provided by their own work. For their own purposes they tended to escalate the acknowledged difficulty and innovation of their art into an unabashedly life-changing moral challenge to the citizenry of the future.

Almost as if in response to their feelings of dislocation in history, Sullivan and Wright were great homogenizers, in fact, glorifiers of nature, natural fact, science, democracy—motifs that run through their quasi-poetic tracts as emblems of the power they would wield over chaos and cant. Sullivan, the more urban of the two, is as much an organicist as Wright, but in practice ascribed less than his student to Whitman's only "those ornaments can be allowed that . . . flow out of the nature of the work and come irrepressibly from it." Indeed, the structure of the mundane buildings Sullivan designed is for the most part unaffected by the heraldic friezes and patches of art-nouveau interlaces which are a decorative tribute to natural growth rather than an integral expression of its economy and energy. The ideal of wholeness to which he aspired, more, in any event, of a psychological than a stylistic simplicity, surfaces

17. Sullivan, indeed, was very fierce on this issue. In his *Kindergarten Chats*, we read: "Current ideas concerning democracy are so vague and current notions concerning man's powers so shapeless, that the man who shall clarify and define, who shall interpret, create and proclaim in the image of Democracy's fair self, will be the destined man of the hour. . . . The world is waiting for such a man as for a Messiah." Yet this does not exempt men from the responsibility of evaluating for themselves, the truths presented to them. Sullivan says: "I subject him [the individual student] to certain experiences and allow the impressions they make on him to infiltrate." Whitman, too, warns against too obedient and single-minded an acceptance of his message: "You shall not look through my eyes either, nor take things from me, / You shall listen to all sides and filter them from your self."

in his writing, though it was never reached in his architecture. In his late years, in *Democracy: A Man-Search*, we read: "These, then, are man's three dreams of power: The dream of work, the dream of might, the dream of cunning. One alone of these dreams is immortal—the dream of work. It is the true dream of creative power. It is the one dream, which includes within itself, the normal ego of the other two. It is the dream that means Life—that invites Life—that invites and guides aright the flow of the All-Life from that dream world which is the real world—the world of the spirit." The narrator of this tome, reflecting the Nietzschean more than the Rabelaisian side of Whitman, chants long lists of factories, hotels, sweat shops, and so on, in put-up-your-dukes prose, "knows all," "feels all," and "hears all." But he is also subject to demented fits of anxiety: "I am thy heart!! Maniac! You have crept into my heart, to ransack it. . . . Speak! Am I not thyself?! No, No!!—Yes, my weaker self. . . ." [18]

No less a synoptic mind, though still prey of similar dialogues and divisions of the self, is Frank Lloyd Wright. At the beginning of his career, in 1896, he enunciated his credo in *Work Song*, extracts from which follow: "I'll live as I work as I am   No work for fashion in sham   . . . My *work* as befitteth a man . . .   I'll work as I think as I am   No thought in fashion for sham   Nor for fortune the jade   Serve vile gods-of-trade   My *thought* as becometh a man   I'll think as I act as I am . . .   My *act* as beseemth a man . . .   I'll act as I'll die as I am . . .   My *life* as betideth a man   *My* life   Aye let come what betideth the man." In Norris Kelly Smith's excellent study we learn that "nothing in Biblical thought [particularly in the meaning of the Hebrew *Dabhar* or "word," which signifies also "to be behind and drive forward"], perhaps, held so central an attraction for the romantics as did its dynamic conception of the word and of the indissoluble unity of word, deed, and self which is what Wright's 'Work Song' is about." It is possible that there would not have been such an almost demonic impulse to bind together principle and actuality if there had not also been such an unremitting sense of cleavage, such a continuous sense of frustration and dilemma in the conditioning of the American artist. Responding to the drag of the protestant ethic, our painters and sculptors intermittently try to assure themselves that what they are really doing is hard, substantial, rewarding work. Architects, in contrast, chafing at their technical status and the immediate practical applicability of their design, poeticize and mythify work, so that it is equated with a disembodied,

18. Louis Sullivan, *Democracy: A Man-Search*.

transcendant spirit. Flowing from the same insecurity, self-legitimization for the two groups moves in opposite directions. Such are the dialectics of a bad artistic conscience.

Americans have little readiness of the heart to come to terms with alienation, to mold out of this negative and lonely perception a style, such as Europeans have molded, that still carries creative value. That is why nature has such an archetypal, resonant presence in American art, unfolding endlessly and nostalgically as one of its grand themes. To fall somehow into step with nature is to regain an integrity before which technology now, and hardship earlier, had opened a bewildering chasm.[19] None of the arts competes with the capacity of architecture to treat physically with nature, and no American architect has even remotely vied with the creator of *Taliesin East* and *Falling Water* in merging shelter with its surroundings. Of his house at Spring Green, Wright says: "I knew well that no house should ever be *on* a hill or *on* anything. It should be *of* the hill. Belonging to it. Hill and house should live together, each the happier for the other. That was the way everything found round about was naturally managed except when man did something." In not wanting to put himself "out of countenance" with southern Wisconsin, Wright initiated one of our most vivid chapters in low-swung aesthetics, going even so far as to deny any validity to the long history of "protruding" artifacts. In his view, the heroism of monuments can only be found wanting when measured against that other heroism—paradoxically diffident in itself—of accepting nature's order. Wright is not implying the surrender of form, but he *is* advocating a sense of form arising out of the extensions, materials, and unpredictabilities of natural growth—like that of a tree. By attempting to liquidate artifice, such an attitude wants to escape any sense of a period style associated with an artifact (although *Taliesin East* was the greatest achievement, and certainly one of the earliest, of American modernism). Not merely is there a free exchange of matter between house and setting, not only do the distinctions between inner and outer space blur at their tangents, but the operative metaphor becomes one of "rootedness" in the earth, occurring unrepeatably, and yet expressing unity with mankind through having been grafted into our common, primordial, life-giving terrain. Moreover, there is a very sug-

19. We need no further evidence of this than Sullivan's remark: "And why is he [the architect] a genius? Because he is a child of nature, single and simple as the weed in the field." To speak of the architect as a "weed" is to impose upon him something of the status of an unwanted loner.

gestive temporizing in what may be called the ontology of the union between site and structure. Does Wright take his inspiration in some metaphorical way from all the appointments of the scene, or does he find subsisting in any one locale living examples of already formulated architectural principles which then become the reflective chorus and complement of the design, the voices of nature, as it were, being given the opportunity of "living up to art"?

In the scheme for *Broadacres City*, Wright is even closer to the spirit of Whitman, and hence to all the confused utopian and communitarian visions of Owen, Fourier, and Noyes, with whom Whitman was in sympathy. Wright plots an agrarian countrywide community, fully interconnected by modern communications and transport, which is dedicated to private, and in great measure, self-reliant, living thus to a kind of freedom not only completely unthinkable in the highly centralized, aggressively productive society of the United States (a society to which he was romantically opposed), but unworkable and contradictory because it provided for no governmental organization and allocation of resources other than those despotically announced by one creator. Just as Wright fallaciously imagined the "collective will" to reside in that of one man, so he postulated an architectural "peaceable kingdom," contemporary in detail but centrifugally preindustrial in goal, spread-eagled into rural antiquity.

No sketch of the Whitmanesque implications in American architecture, finally, could account for its proper plucky climax without attending to the phenomenal scansion of Buckminster Fuller, a builder forging into one technotronic "poetry" whole disciplines such as economy, engineering, and philosophy. Scion of an old New England family, once closely associated with the transcendentalists, Fuller is a realist whose utter pragmatism never ceases to be far fetched. Unlike Wright, who frequently worked as a luxury architect for upper-class clients, Fuller is a planner and inventor seeking complete control amidst the most corporate patronage. For Fuller, the major task is very simply "the direct application of highest potential of scientific advantage toward advancement of world living standards." With his greatest faith placed, not in genius, but in human intelligence, Fuller "promulges" the material suffrage of all, developed and undeveloped peoples, in a world consortium of services made possible through ever more condensed, economical, and efficient technical systems. His is nothing less than a crash program for survival, a race against time to improve global ecological balances, conceiving man's interaction with his environment in the foreshortened perspective of a ballistics expert.

Fuller, more than any other American visual and probably literary artist, other than Whitman, sees "nature" as a cosmological, noninstantaneous motley of reciprocal energy patterns, which man abets by his ability to generalize his anti-entropic, that is, his matter-contracting, function in the overall field of things. In other words, he gains more and more knowledge of his inadvertent and unconscious, but crucial, involvement in all life, and by putting this knowledge to work he insures the performance of every constituent, and thereby his own existence. He says that "generalization in a literary sense means that you are trying to cover too much territory with some statement." However, "the scientific meaning is precise: it means the discovery and statement of a principle that holds true without exceptions." Guided by this definition, he isolates the most relevant principle as man's capacity to do "more with less" [20]—or, to put it differently, the ideological fulcrum of current technological development. This accelerating process has no trouble justifying itself socioeconomically as the major conservator of diminishing resources and the enemy of material waste. In Fuller's perhaps unconscious view, however, it also possesses moral implications (being so much in accord with the protestant ethic) and aesthetic consequences, for it dovetails with the basic tendencies of modern art, at present typified by minimal sculpture.

"Transegrity," "dymaxion," "synergetic"—these neologistic slogans figure conspicuously in the predictive code language whereby Fuller elides use into his elegant, crystalline geodesic domes. Their weight and opacity decrease proportionately in ratio to the increase of their mass. Each is a demonstration of how a building principle can make a shell structure enormously extendable at minimal cost, and at the same time perpetuate a symbolism of the building as a molecular structure, that is, nothing less than a basic constructive block for life itself. Not by their grandeur (though they can be leviathan in size), not by their intricacy or picturesqueness, but by their presumptive, obsessional logic, they impress as the

20. Fuller's language, however, can hardly be taken as an application of this dictum. Reyner Banham, an admirer of the master's comic and often obscurantist jargon, reports that "talking to University College on his last visit to London (before 1963), he [Fuller] involved himself in a twenty-minute relative clause about bird ecology, in the course of which he came up with '. . . and the male birds fly off to sweep out areas of maximum anticipated metabolic advantage.' At which point he paused just long enough to scrutinize what he had said and added 'Worms.' . . ." "Dymaxicrat," *Arts Magazine*, XXXVIII (October, 1963), 68.

memorable outpouring of one creative man. The smaller of these stand-ardized monuments to intelligence can be, and have been, deposited from the skies, as if by a pragmatic God in the shape of a helicopter. Despite their function, often extremely prosaic or matter-of-fact—emergency housing or temporary exhibition centers—they resemble unidentified flying objects roosting improbably in industrial locales that are suddenly made to resemble a bumbling and ham-fisted past. Yet, anatomical in appearance, concerned above all with sealing and packaging (air flow systems, adapt-able heating, light grading), they make remarkably livable and self-sus-taining shelters from every point of view except the psychological.

For these cornerless, light-filled volumes, which may house and manage all the accoutrements of living, reject what is most important to an inhabitant of a building—to feel at home. Unlike Wright, whose every stone evinced personality, although the created aggregate perhaps side-stepped certain physical needs, Fuller's domes satisfy all habitation or functional requirements, but lack personal accent. Moreover, they are deliberately provisional, prefabricated. It's a portable, on-the-go archi-tecture, multipurpose, but never individuated despite innumerable modi-fications. Their trend, ultimately, is to dematerialize the physical para-phernalia of living. Mankind may be very reasonably protected from the elements, but only at the cost of becoming a race of campers.

If Fuller himself feels no problem of identity and unity, both these being effected by the "truth value" of his design philosophy, his architec-ture is a very homeless phenomenon indeed. His presence, in the end, is ambiguous. Doubtless his work must be considered a critique of earlier planning, but he avoids the shaping of space which is one of the justifi-cations of planning. Insulation is an important issue for him because of the outer pollution brought about by the technology he upholds. In addition, it is not clear whether in his view social classes, individual ownership, and conventional politics have eventually to be abolished, or whether artistic creativity itself is so local in relation to urgent and flammable world problems that anything short of his "total," "omnidirectional" solu-tion-field is irrelevant. To grant him this aim is to envisage a politicization of architecture not without alarming aspects. We know that Fuller, alone among the major visionaries of American art, has collaborated with the government on strictly military projects and that he is prominent in giving serious consideration to the necessities of the "third world." Can anyone tell us if he is a believer in God, or antagonistic to all religion, antimaterialist or materialist incarnate? His view of history, less naively

benign than Whitman's, is not prepared to tolerate the validity of his-
torically rooted aspirations to the good life that may differ from his own.
In his remarkable book, *No More Second Hand God*, Fuller writes:
"When the Almighty happened to bemuse his wisdom with playing
shoot-the-works, he opened with one hand the hot valve of absolute
energy and with the other the cold valve of absolute time." Fuller does
not apparently subscribe to Yeats's "bitter dream of limitless energy,"
but he does indicate that "man on earth" must either adopt dymaxion
thinking and thus reach utopia (which will utterly change his humanity),
or choose the only other alternative—oblivion. He calls us to an imperious
tune, and no one knows if it is being played by a prince or a democrat.

How astonishing and varied, then, are the artistic accessories to the
fact of Whitman. Though much of what has happened recently stems
from, or is in reaction to, European vitalism, the latter itself is much
indebted to *Leaves of Grass*, one of the first accomplishments of American
artistic culture to become part of the Western heritage. I have outlined
some of its repercussions among our artists, initially in terms of their
psychic life, the creative processes or attitudes, and the contradictions it
prompted in their awareness of themselves. If nothing else, Whitman, or
his legacy, was productive insofar as his heirs could imaginatively surmount
or subvert it.

What happens, I think, as we look into those careers, or rather, the
way their protagonists polemicize them, is the collapse of most individual
anxieties into a larger continuity of issues concerned with how the world
is to be viewed, and with human life as affected by art. Whitman's poetry
can be seen as a kind of railroad roundhouse where the idea of a bucolic
landscape gets switched to a concept of a mental table of the future, or
where perceived time and space are rerouted into a seasonless rebuke of
history itself. Whitman's oscillations between humble observer and God-
like creator, his ecstatic but mongrelized reconstruction of language, suggest, despite sometimes imposed resolutions, a loss of equilibrium. There
is about his progeny, as also about those artists who have responded
sensitively to the American experience in general, a Whitmanesque striving to regain balance, a will to reach the one in the many, the many in
the one.

Edwin Haviland Miller

The Radical Vision
of Whitman and Pollock

Walt Whitman and Jackson Pollock are undoubtedly our most radical artists. Whitman and Pollock altered the American landscape and American consciousness fundamentally. Whitman wrenched and twisted traditional poetry and metrics to accommodate his vision and his personality. Pollock destroyed Renaissance and cubistic perspectives and planes, and refused to abide by the limitations of canvas and established easel technique in order to force the pictorial medium to subserve his vision and his personality. Both were iconoclasts and egomaniacs, and both, although solitary and withdrawn persons, became personality cults. Such was the uniqueness of their art that their imitators proved them inimitable.

Whitman and Pollock so outraged the establishment and the public that from the beginning they received the attention they deserved for the wrong reasons. *Leaves of Grass,* an oversized book with a peculiar title when it appeared anonymously in 1855, provoked readers. According to one newspaper it had all leaves except fig leaves, and shortly Whitman, with his Olympian face, became "the dirty old man," although in some respects he was more virginal than most virgins. Pollock was termed "Jack the Ripper," a nasty, but clear epithet which unconsciously recognizes the painter's erotic power and his rape of the visual sense. In the eyes of some early critics and some modern schoolteachers, Whitman abandoned rhymes and meter because he was incapable of following the rules and placed whatever came into his head on paper without thought or art. Pollock, the hostile averred, spattered paint on a canvas as some people do on floors for a Cape Cod effect or as children do when they do not want to draw or paint.

We all know that Whitman could write conventional poetry—the public has always admired one of his lesser achievements, "O Captain! My Captain!"—but his genius was not at home inside convention. We should know by this time that Whitman meticulously revised his poems before and after publication. Even if his manuscripts had not been preserved, it takes little acumen to realize that "Song of Myself" and his other great poems did not fall into order upon the page as accidents. Such "accidents" happen only to genius. Similarly, no Sunday painter can stumble into the complex order of "Blue Poles" [Plate 7]. Amateurs and children, as we all should know, can make botches that resemble Rohrschach tests, but ordinarily they mix the botches with poorly drawn houses, trees, and people, for they soon learn to imitate the stereotypes and visual limitations of the myopic adult world. Although Pollock's canvases may impress the amateur as a series of accidents, the expert opinion of William Rubin is closer to the truth: *"The finished picture was not made up of accidents but of responses to them."* [1] Which is quite a different matter, for Rubin correctly emphasizes artistic control that is rational and emotional, conscious and unconscious. What is childlike in Pollock's art—and like Whitman and most artists he evokes the polymorphous landscape of childhood—is beyond the emotional needs of one who still dwells in the paradise which the mature artist must seek in nostalgic evocation. Art for the child is primarily diversion; for the mature man it is "remembrance of things past."

When Whitman and Pollock "undrape," to use one of the poet's key words, they unsettle and arouse anxieties which are released in vituperative assaults upon the integrity of the artists. In his desire to maintain his vulnerable security in an uncertain and contradictory world, man wants the comfort that the dogmas of convention accord, the illusion of order that existing forms provide against impending chaos, and a manageable and familiar size or scale that poses no threat to his feelings of dominancy. As Emerson sensed long ago, man prefers the dead sight of the past to living sight. Thus he resists the visions of innovative "see-ers" like Whitman and Pollock, until with understanding and the passage of time the new way of seeing is properly aged, formlessness becomes form through familiarity and imitation, and the monumental scale no longer seems intimidating.

1. William Rubin, "Jackson Pollock and the Modern Tradition, Part II," *Artforum*, V (March, 1967), 31.

When the American cultural revolution occurred in the 1850s, and *The Scarlet Letter, Moby-Dick, Walden,* and *Leaves of Grass* appeared within five years, artists separated themselves from English models as completely as the nation had shed English tyranny almost seventy-five years earlier. With the possible exception of Hawthorne's romance, although his symbolic allegory is successfully Americanized, these works almost cannot be classified in terms of traditional genres because the authors dismissed, with unconcealed glee, the conventions of prose and poetry. It has become a truism that most great American art seems to have no antecedents. It is an orphan art. It is the appropriate expression of a people who often like to believe that the nation is beyond history, that the present and the future have no parentage. Paradoxically, the nation almost always rejects its artistic children, who thereupon assume the Ishmael role characteristic of our literature since the appearance of our first literary and mythic hero, Cooper's Natty Bumppo. Eventually artists are accepted, almost like prodigal sons, by forgiving parents who reluctantly and belatedly bestow praise usually given first in other lands.

Artists, of course, are not so ahistorical as the nation pretends to be. Years of study and discipline are part of what they may later consider "compulsory miseducation" in the tradition. When, like Thoreau, they follow a "different drummer," they consciously and deliberately overturn worn out, obsolete rules no more relevant to contemporary life than feudalism is to individualism. However, the artistic new "order" is not a *tabula rasa;* rather, it is a modern conversion of, or reversion to, an older, more "primitive" tradition which implicitly recognizes the unity of "the savage mind" that the artificialities of civilization fragment because of the rigid separation of body and head, irrationality and reason, particularization and conceptualization. Art demonstrates that mankind moves forward only to retreat periodically to the ancient fountains, or moves in search of new-old wisdom, as Faust does in the second part of Goethe's great drama.

Whitman, like Allen Ginsberg and his followers in our time, sought to reestablish the oral tradition of bardic poetry, not only to return the poet to the center of the stage from the wings where a pragmatic age of pragmatic prose had consigned him, but also to purge the poetic line of the effeminate mellifluousness of Longfellow and Tennyson. The era sang soulfully and genteelly of disembodied spirits without genitals—a cultural emasculation presided over by the good Queen Victoria, a living example of the "good" mother that terrifies the supposedly stronger sex. Whitman undraped the body electric in a cadence that owes more to the Bible than to anatomy textbooks. His much-maligned catalogs are rhythmically closer to the lists of ships in Homer and to the genealogies in the Old Testament than to city directories or inventories of merchandise. His radical journey of self-exploration leads him to the depths of the self and the race, not in the diction of anthropologists or the early psychologists, but in the intonations of biblical innocence: "There was a child went forth every day"—a line which may violate the rules of scansion but does not violate itself.

Pollock has been said to be an urban painter, as Whitman is alleged to be an urban poet. But such rubrics misuse biographical facts in order to offer nonexplanations. It would be just as meaningful, and in final analysis meaningless, to call Pollock a Western painter because he was born in an Indian outpost (Cody, Wyoming), spent his formative years in Arizona, and drew upon Aztec symbols and Indian totems in his pictures. Regardless of place of birth and regardless of the mature years spent in New York artistic circles, Pollock's subject matter is neither the urban landscapes of Hopper, Marin, and Feininger, nor the pictorializations of Remington, Russell, and Biddle. His landscapes—"One" or "Autumn Rhythm" [Plate 6]—exist outside of particularized space and chronological time. They are closer to cave paintings than to the murals of Biddle or Orozco. Pollock's paintings "speak," if they speak at all to spectators, in a personal but universal sign language, not in a public but time-limited (contemporaneous) language.

Although he freely acknowledged indebtedness to the theories of Freud and Jung, he translated their formulations into a pictorial vocabulary relevant to his vision and his inner drama. Almost alone among American artists Pollock utilizes Indian symbols, not to depict the white rape of the red man, but to fuse savage and civilized man. Writers like Cooper, Melville, and Robert Lowell enter neither the white nor the Indian consciousness when they speak, however movingly, about a guilt which few Americans are willing to share. Theirs is a moral posture—of mental, not bodily, consciousness—and they are outsiders, like George Caitlin, who rarely married his empathy to his limited pictorial skill. Pollock's paintings may violate academic rules of realism and the public's craving for naturalism, but, like Whitman's primitive, unmetrical lines, they are true to themselves and to the artist's encompassing vision—to the "hidden order of art" in the unconscious.

It is not necessary to assert a "hidden order," although that approach is especially applicable to the two artists, in order to defend their seeming formlessness. Form in life and art is an order, a norm, to the conservative mentality an absolute, which has achieved wide acceptance over a period of time. It freezes life and art into a mold which becomes life-denying in its denial of flux and change, but which provides a consoling illusion of permanence or stasis. When the norm is challenged by social unrest or by artistic exploration, immediately there are warnings, in the hushed tones of Cassandra, of chaos, anarchy, formlessness. Change or a void triggers emotions and arouses anxieties which have been cradled in a reassuring illusion. Yet the so-called "absence of form" in Whitman and Pollock can be explained and defended as a modernized realism, with an indebtedness to Lucretius and Montaigne as well as to primitivism, which is faithful, too faithful for many tastes, to human nature, to external nature, and to the social and intellectual conventions of the contemporary world.

In their use of form, these two artists recognize the omnipresence of flux—that the ceaseless change has its own order. Because the mind prefers simplifications, human nature is reduced to types, humours, character sketches, in other words, to a consistent, predictable pattern which is blatantly false to the inconsistencies, the fluctuating moods and opinions, and the contradictions of man. His life becomes a story with a beginning, a middle, and a conclusion, in which climaxes and anticlimaxes are achieved by exaggerating minor fluctuations into major movements which add interest and zest to the tale. Rather than the "disorderly" life of which Whitman sings, life is packaged or embalmed, so that neat conclusions, intellectual oversimplifications, can be drawn. "Song of Myself" was, on its appearance in 1855, a shocking poem not simply because Whitman aggressively asserted his self-importance, but because he introduced a new form in which to depict the "disorderly," contradictory life of a self-styled "rough" and a "kosmos." Lines vary in length, the 1336 lines are not arbitrarily divided, and, perhaps by accident, there is no period at the end of the last line. Yet lines vary according to changing moods; climaxes are not artificially created or indicated, and the movement continues beyond the terminal line of the poem.

I bequeath myself to the dirt to grow from the grass I love,
If you want me again look for me under your bootsoles.

You will hardly know who I am or what I mean,
But I shall be good health to you nevertheless,
And filter and fibre your blood.

Failing to fetch me at first keep encouraged,
Missing me one place search another,
I stop some where, waiting for you

Similarly, the group of poems known as "Calamus" relates no consecutive tale of love won, love lost, and love regained. The poems fluctuate with the swings of a man who is simultaneously an artist and a lover, who at one moment is ready to sublimate his unreturned passion in poetry and at the next is ready to abandon poetry in order to be with his beloved. He enjoys love and its loss, for without love there is no physical gratification, but without loss there is no occasion for poetry. "Calamus" reflects the flux inherent in the two conflicting roles the artist-lover plays in a drama that can have no clear-cut conclusion.

The endless gyrations of Pollock's over-all canvases are the visual counterparts of Whitman's verbal transitoriness. Just as Whitman's catalogs move the eye and the mind from one object to the next without regard to similarities or familiar rational relationships, so Pollock's restless lines of paint ignore the four corners of the canvas and refuse to fall into the customary patterns of representational art. The eye of the spectator seeks resolution, focus, a center of interest, but he remains frustrated until (or unless) he sheds the blinders of convention. Even Pollack's color mixtures refuse to provide the usual harmony, for they are ever changing, incongruously blending, and then emerging elsewhere for no apparent reason. The difficulty the spectator has is not with Pollock's abstractness but with his fidelity to nature. To confirm the realism we have only to look at the branches of a leafless tree: they twist aimlessly, thicken and thin out, form patternless patterns of motion that rarely provide the eye with the rest it seeks. Or if we examine photographs of the ocean floor, we find strange forms that defy classical order, patterns that resemble not at all Byzantine arrangements, and conglomerative colors unrelated to the orderly colors of representational or impressionistic art. When Pollock depicts spring, he does not have a tree or a flower about to burst into life, in pale green; he fills the canvas with vibrant, restless bunches or drops of warm colors which have no discernible configuration except that of eternal motion or eternal rebirth. There is an erotic gaiety in the painting which is not too different from Whitman's description of another season: "A show of summer softness. . . . a contact of something unseen. . . . an amour of the light and air." Both Whitman and Pollock are incapable of the romantic gloom and the intellectual falsification of such a line as "April is the cruellest month." For birth, human and nonhuman, is pain as well as joy.

The absence in their works of the usual cerebral differentiations in the human and natural landscapes records truthfully not only the see-saws of man's emotions and the unending motion of the earth that endureth forever, but also the collapse of a hierarchical society and cosmos. Democracy had toppled aristocratic classes and manners; industrialism had opened the closed feudalistic order; scientific theories had cast doubt upon the hierarchies of religion as well as upon earlier scientific schematizations. Whitman and Pollock are artists of the new-old universe based on the flux and limitless space of Einstein and the neurotic rhythms of the maturational theories of Freud. Thus, they are in one sense artists of dissolution and in another sense harbingers of a synthesis struggling for birth. Whitman's art has been more convincing than his prophecies, for his art has the order of the unconscious, but his prognostications are dubious intellectualizations of emotional needs. Camaraderie is a desirable goal, but not when it is marred by homosexual wish-fulfillment. Because the brush speaks in lines and colors, Pollock was under no obligation, either personal or verbal, to reduce his creed to words. He could paint his anguish in the works of the 1940s and his joyful resolution in "Autumn Rhythm" (1950) and "Blue Poles" (1953) [Plates 6 and 7]. He could even dance gaily to the abyss in an ambiguously lovely painting like "The Deep," which Frank O'Hara characterizes as "an abyss of glamour encroached upon by a flood of innocence" [2] but which may also be the pictorial equivalent of Whitman's carol in "When Lilacs Last in the Dooryard Bloom'd":

> Prais'd be the fathomless universe,
> For life and joy, and for objects and knowledge
>   curious,

2. Frank O'Hara, *Jackson Pollock* (New York: George Braziller, Inc., 1959), p. 31.

And for love, sweet love—but praise! praise! praise!
For the sure-enwinding arms of cool-enfolding death.

The American adventure from the very beginning in the seventeenth-century colonies has been epic in its scale, in the heroic expansion from the Atlantic to the Pacific Oceans, in its dreams of "manifest destiny," in its abiding faith that it can create within its vast boundaries a new Eden. Americans "think big" and "talk big"—in the "American dream," advertisements and tall tales, schemes for universal education and the eradication of poverty, and even in their art. "Song of Myself" and Pollock's "One" (measuring almost nine by eighteen feet) are examples of thinking and talking big. Although they are epic in scale, they make personal or lyrical statements, just as the American dream is a collective wish for self-glorification or for rugged, but sometimes anarchistic, individualism. This contradiction, artistic and cultural, attests to our uniqueness, or even our modernity, but it illustrates a conflict that has not as yet been successfully resolved. Where Homer recalls an historic event in which aristocratic heroes reflect racial grandeur, Whitman recalls his own history and asserts the heroic potentiality of the common American man. Where Michelangelo draws upon Judeo-Christian myths and superhuman heroes, Pollock "writes" in a personal vocabulary without obvious syntactical and cultural antecedents. The lyrical epics or epical lyrics of Whitman and Pollock are extraordinary artistic creations, but they speak too immediately and personally to a people which often uses its Gargantuan creations and edenic theories to hide from self-criticism and painful self-analysis.

"Song of Myself" and "One" depict, as American art has since the days of James Fenimore Cooper and Thomas Cole, the solitary individual in an overwhelming environment which threatens to outrun his tools of mastery and to engulf him. At the same time the two works assert, perhaps overassert in a characteristically American fashion, the power of the individual ego to subdue space or at least to reduce it to manageable dimensions. Although Whitman's "kosmos" flows on with a spatial and temporal freedom that almost takes the hero out of space and time, he never loses his identity or control. He is most emphatically "Walt Whitman, an American, one of the roughs, a kosmos." At the same time, the "I" is companioned by the "you," the audience—from the second line, "And what I assume you shall assume," to the last line, "I stop some where, waiting for you." As Rubin points out,[3] Pollock's scale also encompasses and absorbs "you." The private vocabulary of lines and colors surrounds the spectator and thrusts him into the center of a figurative universe where he is master and interpreter—but a sheltered child, too.

There is duplicity here. The erotic bond between the artist and his audience is wish-fulfillment (an artifact remains an artifact) and reflects the impersonality that even art cannot escape in the age of the dynamo. The seductive approach of the artist is inadequate compensation for the cultural chill. In lovely lines Whitman makes over the landscape in the image of his own amorous propensities, which stem from personal frustrations:

> Press close barebosomed night! Press close
>   magnetic nourishing night!
> Night of south winds! Night of the large few
>   stars!
> Still nodding night! Mad naked summer night!
>
> Smile O voluptuous coolbreathed earth!
> Earth of the slumbering and liquid trees!
> Earth of departed sunset! Earth of the mountains
>   misty-topt!
> Earth of the vitreous pour of the full moon just
>   tinged with blue!
> Earth of shine and dark mottling the tide of the
>   river!
> Earth of the limpid gray of clouds brighter and
>   clearer for my sake!
> Far-swooping elbowed earth! Rich apple-blossomed
>   earth!
> Smile, for your lover comes!

There is perhaps overemphasis upon the self when things are no longer things but narcissistic reflections. In the hundreds of poems written by the man who liked to proclaim himself the poet of democracy, no one

3. Rubin, p. 36: "The big Pollocks are related to the late Monets not only in aspects of their plasticity but in their *intimacy*, a quality they share with the wall-size pictures of Rothko, Newman and Still. Unlike the *Guernica* and the monumental art of the past, they are meant. . . . for private apartments and they address the spectator on an individual basis."

emerges as an identifiable individual. Whitman's people are not even granted the dignity of a name, but are reduced to gestures characteristic of their trades and pursuits. They are objects in an egocentric landscape. Naturally these muscular gestures are not capable of dialogue. Whitman replaces meaningful social interaction with a lovely, seductive monologue, although his art is intended to create the illusion of a dialogue. The reader, like the poet, however, talks only to himself.

Like Whitman, Pollock denies the spectator the pleasures of a specific flower, tree, or terrain. Particulars are generalized because, as he acknowledged, it was not his intention to dwell upon the external world: "The modern artist, it seems to me, is working and expressing an inner world—in other words—expressing the energy, the motion, and other inner forces." [4] Consequently, when people emerge from his lines of paint, only outlines establish their presence. As in dreams sexual identification is not easily made—even in "Male and Female" [Plate 5]. Pollock's figures are usually recognizable archetypes, but we love and hate, marry and bury, people, not archetypes. Neither Pollock nor Whitman permits us to empathize with, or even to identify, Tom or Jane. We are fettered with seductive words or colors to the artist's inner world, to his narcissism, to his fears of people and personal involvements. Although we share the same inner world, narcissism, and fears, and although we share the same (unstated) hunger to be incorporated into the world, there are pleasures in external reality, human and nonhuman, which these two artists do not reflect. The great art of Pollock and Whitman tends to lead toward reconciliation with permanent estrangement.

The compulsive dwelling upon the inner landscape—the absence of human and natural referents, the tendency of the artist, like the child in his egocentric world, to dominate all relationships and to make the world over in terms of his needs—clearly establishes the fact that Whitman and Pollock composed their autobiographies in their respective mediums. Despite some of his foolish prose statements about his intentions, Whitman knew what he was doing when he titled his greatest poem "Song of Myself." Pollock was not speaking idly when he said, "The source of my painting is the unconscious," or when he observed in an interview: "Painting is self-discovery. Every good artist paints what he is." [5] It is not necessary—and indeed it would be futile—to concern ourselves with

4. Pollock, as quoted by Francis V. O'Connor, *Jackson Pollock* (New York: The Museum of Modern Art, 1967), p. 80.
5. Pollock, as quoted by O'Connor, pp. 40, 73.

autobiographical details, for both artists extrapolated from the unconscious and deliberately submerged specific details in what Whitman terms "faint clews & indirections." But a portrait in broad strokes emerges.

Both were isolates, solitary singers in the vast but lonely American environment where artists are regarded as deviants. Because tradition provided inadequate vehicles for the expression of their estrangement, they were orphans in art as well as in life. Without external props, they turned in or, like Narcissus, bent down to examine the reflection; "self-discovery" meant painful journeys to the primordial sources of life and art—the mysteries of birth and of the child's emergence into light and his subsequent traumas. "The Sleepers" is an extraordinary hallucinated revelation of Whitman's confrontation with the unresolved conflicts of his life. In Pollock's canvases of the 1940s, hidden fears—overpowering eyes, strange birds, webs, humans in contorted postures—come into view and then retreat into the lines from which they momentarily emerge. As in "The Sleepers" this is the terrain of dreams. Pollock's "Male and Female" [Plate 5] should no doubt be subtitled "Father and Mother." The two figures almost (but, significantly, do not) fuse in coitus, for a strange diamond-shaped obstacle absorbs the penis and prevents penetration. Two similar objects protect the breasts, which, with the rounded (perhaps pregnant) belly, are the focal points of the canvas. The woman's mouth is alarmingly open—to devour the male, both father and child—and rests at the top of a phallic totem, which is filled with seemingly meaningless numbers in a childlike scrawl. The male is masculine when viewed from the right, but feminine when viewed from the left. The sexual confusion recalls the child's confusion of sexual roles and his own identity as well as his Oedipal ambivalences. Snakes, weblike feet, circles, fiery explosions, as well as the blues and blacks, are more turbulent expressions of the night fears Whitman describes with deceptive simplicity in a sequence in "The Sleepers," in which the "I" of the poems assumes various sexual roles in the primal act:

> I am she who adorned herself and folded her
>   hair expectantly,
> My truant lover has come and it is dark.
>
> Double yourself and receive me darkness,
> Receive me and my lover too . . . . he will not
>   let me go without him.

I roll myself upon you as upon a bed. . . .
    I resign myself to the dusk.

He whom I call answers me and takes the place
    of my lover,
He rises with me silently from the bed.

Darkness you are gentler than my lover. . . . his
    flesh was sweaty and panting,
I feel the hot moisture yet that he left me.

My hands are spread forth. . . . I pass them in
    all directions,
I would sound up the shadowy shore to which
    you are journeying.

Dore Ashton has written perceptively of Pollock: "The basic quality was an insistent stress on the curving form—the womb or cocoon enclosure. Even in his late 'drip' paintings this persistent instinct for circular enclosures exists." [6] Thus "The Deep" [Plate 8] is more than an "abyss of glamour": it is the ravishing beauty of the eternal womb from which man emerges and to which he returns—in short, paradise regained. It should be scarcely surprising that Pollock found Albert Ryder "the only American master who interests me," [7] for that lonely, introspective artist was haunted by mysterious seas in which hollowed-out boats (cradles-coffins) rocked. The rhythms of Ryder's (and Pollock's) paint resembles the rocking motion of the participles in Whitman's "Out of the Cradle Endlessly Rocking," which depicts the boy-poet's introduction to loss and finally to death, which is rebirth, or, more accurately, return to the mother.

That strong and delicious word which, creeping
    to my feet,
(Or like some old crone rocking the cradle,
    swathed in sweet garments, bending aside,)
The sea whisper'd me.

6. Dore Ashton, *The Unknown Shore: A View of Contemporary Art* (Boston: Little, Brown & Company, 1962), p. 45.
7. Pollock, as quoted by O'Connor, p. 32.

Our greatest elegy, "When Lilacs Last in the Dooryard Bloom'd," moves from the particular loss of a great president to a universal statement in a "carol," the song the mother sings to her child:

> Lost in the loving floating ocean of thee,
> Laved in the flood of thy bliss O death.

The "God" with whom the "I" in "Passage to India" unites is a bisexual deity:

> lave me all over,
> Bathe me O God in thee, mounting to thee,
> I and my soul to range in range of thee.

The personal quest (the autobiography) is inevitably reflected in artistic technique and esthetic theory. Pollock's canvases enclose the viewer in a kind of cocoon. Whitman's lines extend beyond the page to touch the reader: "I was chilled with the cold types and cylinders and wet paper between us." Or in those familiar lines which have excited amorousness in some readers and repelled others:

> Camerado, this is no book,
> Who touches this touches a man.

Whitman refuses to grant readers the intellectual and emotional distance (and safety) they desire, and Pollock closes in upon the viewers with an urgency and immediacy that people do not expect in the environment of a museum.

Whitman was the first American artist to acknowledge the eroticism of art ("I hear the trained soprano. . . . she convulses me like the climax of my love-grip") and to assert unequivocally the orgiastic sources of his poetry. In an era in which proper Americans said "limbs" instead of "legs" and clothed the limbs of pianos in virginal yard goods, he admitted to "singing the phallus." In "Spontaneous Me," which at its first appearance bore an appropriately risible and genital title, "Bunch Poem," he writes:

> The real poems, (what we call poems being
>   merely pictures,)
> The poems of the privacy of the night, and of
>   men like me,
> The poem, drooping shy and unseen, that I always
>   carry, and that all men carry,
> (Know, once for all, avowed on purpose, wherever
>   are men like me, are our lusty, lurking,
>   masculine, poems,) . . . .

"Trickle Drops," like so many of the other "Calamus" poems, depicts the masturbatory fantasies of the lover-poet, who proceeds to equate onanism and art:

> O drops of me! trickle, slow drops,
> Candid, from me falling—drip, bleeding drops,
> From wounds made to free you whence you were
>   prisoned,
> From my face—from my forehead and lips,
> From my breast—from within where I was concealed—
>   Press forth, red drops—confession drops,
> Stain every page—stain every song I sing,
>   every word I say, bloody drops,
> Let them know your scarlet heat—let them
>   glisten,
> Saturate them with yourself, all ashamed and wet,
> Glow upon all I have written or shall write,
>   bleeding drops,
> Let it all be seen in your light, blushing drops.

The overman in "Song of Myself" is an Americanized Zeus as he bestrides the "kosmos"—or a wonderfully comic instance of an American "thinking big":

> On women fit for conception I start bigger and nimbler babes,
> This day I am jetting the stuff of far more arrogant republics.

In other works the poet declares the artist (himself) the impregnator of democracy, which, interestingly enough, is either a woman or, more usually and Oedipally, a mother. Whitman's political views are not un-related to his personal conflicts.

In discussing Pollock's "insistent stress on the curving form," Ashton neglects the vertical thrusts of the phallic totems in works like "Male and Female" (1942) and especially "Blue Poles" (1953) [Plates 5 and 7]. Of the latter work O'Hara rhapsodizes with an intuitive feeling too seldom encountered in art criticism:

> Blue Poles is our Raft of the Medusa and our Embarkation for Cytherea in one. I say our, because it is the drama of an American conscience, lavish, bountiful and rigid. It contains everything within itself, begging no quarter: a world of sentiment implied, but denied; a map of sensual freedom, fenced; a careening licentiousness, guarded by eight totems native to its origins. . . . What is expressed here is not only basic to his work as a whole, but it is final.[8]

Whether we agree with O'Hara's response in every detail is of little moment, since the immense canvas invites and absorbs multiple responses. O'Hara, however, does not account adequately for the harmony Pollock achieves in this work. Here the masculine and feminine lines or symbols fuse because Pollock has successfully fused the bisexual tendencies of his (and human) nature. In "Male and Female" [Plate 5] the insistent totems and peculiar, dream-like shapes divide rather than unite the two fractured figures, for the artist himself has not come to terms with the fracturing effects of the Oedipal conflict. The blue phallus in "Male and Female" is denied consummation, and it is probably (unconsciously) no mistake that blue poles in the later work dance Dionysiacally. "Male and Female" disturbs the spectator because it stirs up deep-seated and repressed fears, but "Blue Poles" [Plate 7] soothes because the lines of paint caress and the powerful arm of the artist guides the viewer gaily in an elegant dance that never ceases. Pollock's graceful leap to affirmation and serenity springs from the erotic culmination of colors bursting into patterns and of lines wiggling sensually to coital fulfillment. Here he achieves personal and artistic resolution.

As Whitman merged person and artifact—"I spring from the pages into your arms"—so Pollock abandoned the easel which not only controls the way paint can be used but also keeps the artist at an arbitrary distance.

8. O'Hara, pp. 30–31.

"On the floor I am more at ease," he declared. "I feel nearer, more a part of the painting, since this way I can walk around it, work from the four sides and literally be *in* the painting." [9] A fascinating series of photographs in Bryan Robertson's study reveals Pollock in the act of painting one of his overall works. With a bucket of paint and a brush or stick, he drops paint on the large rectangular canvas tacked to the floor. Above it he stands, his eyes haunted and his body rigid with concentrated energy about to explode. The loneliness is awesome, but body and mind have fused as the orphan-artist is about to stain a universe into life with brushes of color. "Stain every page—stain every song I sing, every word, I say, bloody drops," Whitman declares. The act of impregnation culminates in the birth of the artifact. For the artist fuses sexual separateness: he is both male and female.

Whitman sounded his "barbaric yawp over the roofs of the world," and the phrase ever since has identified the self-styled "rough." But Whitman's "yawp" is elegant rather than "barbaric." The line that follows the reverbations of "my barbaric yawp" is a delicate diminuendo: "The last scud of day holds back for me." The "rough," despite his overasserted masculinity, is the master-mistress of the exquisite effects of a miniaturist (or lyricist), as Pollock's works are gigantic miniatures in a unique "handwriting," to borrow Robertson's felicitous term. Pollock's lines of paint move with a restless muscular energy more characteristic of the restless male than of the (relatively) quiescent female, but, as Sam Hunter observes, "his bursting masculinity had to contend not only with itself, but with a delicate and often exquisite sensibility in line and color." [10] What Hunter describes is both a cultural and personal conflict. America, true to its frontier spirit perhaps, has stridently opted for red-blooded boys and red-blooded men—absolutes impossible of precise or even imprecise definition. Concerned about their suspect role in a society which worships action, our artists have sought to justify themselves and to escape the onus of effeminacy—from Emerson's search for a "virile" style to Hemingway's hirsute code. Both the culture and its artists reveal a deep-rooted anxiety characteristic of a society and a people "on the make." Pollock's muscularity and Whitman's obsessive phallicism illustrate the

9. Bryan Robertson, *Jackson Pollock* (New York: Harry N. Abrams, Inc., 1960), p. 193.

10. Sam Hunter, "Jackson Pollock," *The Museum of Modern Art Bulletin,* XXIV, No. 2 (1956–1957), 9.

conflict, for both seek to hide their shrinking and timid temperaments behind a virile façade.

Yet great art successfully blends, as Herman Hesse notes, the male and female components, strength and delicacy, mind and heart, reason and instinct, conscious and unconscious. Just as secret primitive rites among males attempt to emulate the fertility of woman, a more envied state than so-called penis envy, artists attempt to bridge the division between the two worlds imposed by biology and to restore the androgynous unity of childhood. This is the Faustian quest.

Whitman and Pollock were untimid explorers both of artistic form and of themselves. Despite the fumbling at the beginning of their careers —the early Whitman was less than mediocre in prose and poetry, and the early Pollock was scarcely the most promising of artists in W. P. A. days— both finally arrived at the necessary critical insight that precedes the translation of vision into art. Both are contemplative artists, and meditation is the subject matter of our art as well as its characteristic "form"—in Herman Melville and Albert Ryder, Thomas Eakins and Emily Dickinson, Henry Adams and Maurice Prendergast, William Faulkner and Morris Graves, Ernest Hemingway and Edward Hopper. These meditations dwell upon the inner landscape, which the American artist has mastered as he has almost invariably failed to subdue the external landscape. In his hands the epic has been lyricized and personalized. Man may never again stop long enough to establish the conceptual and cultural foundations upon which the Homeric epic rests, but the artist will contest the depersonalization of technocracy with his lyrical affirmation. Perhaps, as Robert Frost observes, man will "be but more free to think/For the one more cast-off shell"—a masculine statement which needs feminine expansion—"free to think and feel." For these American artists—and especially Whitman and Pollock—have in their meditations "written" with a delicacy that may charm the mind but solaces the heart.

Robert Duncan

Changing Perspectives
in Reading Whitman

When I was invited to participate in this celebration of Whitman's sesquicentennial, I had thought that I would write a formal lecture, a companion piece for a lecture I had done in 1965 in homage to Dante upon his seventh centennial. Whitman, like Dante, was a poet central to my thought, a perennial source from which my own art as a poet drew. And there were formal parallels that might have been made: Whitman, like Dante, projected a poem central to his civilization and his vision of the ground of ultimate reality—*Leaves of Grass*, like the *Divina Commedia*, being not an epic narrative but the spiritual testament of a self-realization. Whitman, as Dante did in his *De Vulgari Eloquentia*, wrote, in the Preface of the 1855 edition of *Leaves of Grass*—to which I would add the essay "Slang in America," written in 1885—a poetics grounded in a science of the language of the common people. Whitman's statement that "view'd freely, the English language is the accretion and growth of every dialect, race, and range of time, and is both the free and compacted composition of all" is directly comparable to Dante's sense of the illustrious vernacular, the language in which the spirit of Man was embodied most wholly; and Whitman's "It is curiously in embryons and childhood, and among the illiterate, we always find the groundwork and start, of this great science, and its noblest products" agrees closely, indeed, with Dante's sense that "our first true speech" is "that to which children are accustomed by those who are about them when they first begin to distinguish words . . . that which we acquire without any rule, by imitating our nurses."

Whitman in *Democratic Vistas*, like Dante in *De Monarchia*, had written a definitive—even *the* definitive—politics of his time ("his time" being the time created in his poetic vision). Whitman, like Dante, had this vision of Time, of Self and World, in his poetic conversion, through the medium of a falling-in-love, where the inspiration of that falling-in-love being never exorcised in a sexual satisfaction, longing had been the seed of a creative desire transforming the inner and outer reality. Freud has made us aware, even wary, of such a process of sublimation, and simple Freudians, those who do not go along with Freud's mythic imagination toward his deeper vision of the work of Eros and Thanatos in Creation, think of sublimation as a removal from the primary genital fact, which is real, a flight from what is sexual and actual into higher thought and abstraction. The generation of poets who were contemporary with psychoanalysis also had a bias against abstraction; Pound, Williams, and we as their progeny have sought to test language, as if many of its functions were unreal or unsound or unsavory, against a control taken, in mimesis of the empiricism presumed in the scientific method, from the observable "objective" world. But I would see the process at work in Dante's and Whitman's falling in love in light of another reading out of Freud, in which Eros and Thanatos are primary, at work in the body of the poem even as they are at work in the body of the man, awakening in language apprehensions of what we call sexuality and spirituality. Parts of language, like parts of the physical body, will be inspired; syllables and words, like cells and organs, will be excited, awakened to the larger identity they belong to.

Longing had been the seed, for Whitman as for Dante, of a creative desire, a new life, transforming the inner and outer reality of a poetic vision. As words belong to language and cells to animal bodies, poets come to belong to a poetry. But, here, just where Dante had begun with the foundation-stone of his *Vita Nuova*, creating in the world of ultimate poetic realities his Beatrice and establishing in the world of actual histories the poetic riddle of that reality, Whitman does not venture. Dante had cast over and through the real the enchantment of a commanding romance; he had established a *locus solus* in the daughter of Folco Portinari, wife of Simone de'Bardi, for the persona of Universal Being. Whitman, again and again, resolves to release man from romantic entanglement. The particularity and uniqueness, the painfulness, of Whitman's Beloved is released into the presence of the Beloved in throngs of men, a vision of democracy in which the Beloved is equally apprehended in all the variety and generative potentiality of mankind.

Inviting as such a fitting of parallels might be, the very fitting misfits.

It is not only that generations of poets over seven hundred years have raised the imagination of the poet Dante again and again, and that our imagination of him has all the resource of that increment of associations, nor that Dante himself drew upon three generations of poets, a tradition in which the Spirit of Romance had grown from the schools of Provence to thirteenth-century Florence, nor that in turn he had a guide in the spirit of Virgil, and with Cavalcanti and Lapo Gianni, he belonged to a school, a "scene" or "movement" of the thirteenth century with advanced ideas about love and the nature of poetry. Whitman too is very much the member of such a movement in poetry in the nineteenth century; he comes to fulfill and he sees himself as fulfilling, as Dante came to fulfill the meaning of the troubadors, the vision of the poet that begins, for Whitman, in Carlyle's *Heroes and Hero-Worship* and passes on through Emerson's writings. We have only to read Whitman's essays on the Bible, on Shakespeare, on the work of his own contemporaries, to realize how firm his grasp is of literary realities; he has here the largeness of mind and at the same time the keenness of perception that Dante has.

But Whitman nowhere presents the architectural ordering of universe and spirit that Dante presents. One had only, with Dante, to present the fittings of parts in a designated passage to arrive at its relevance; the design of reality in Dante was established in orders given and giving order to one's thought if it be but appropriate to the object. Whitman presents no such a settled business. He is the grand proposer of questions not to be settled, the poet of unsettling propositions. And as I worked on this previous to the lecture my notes became very dense, and in that density the sense of the task of unwinding the threads grew—out of hand. The *Leaves of Grass* in its nine editions grows, not toward a definitive architecture, but as a man grows, composed and recomposed, in each phase immediate and complete, but unsatisfied. It was my impulse then when I came to the lecture itself, as now again in preparing the lecture for its written version to be published, to let impulse and association enter into the composition, the talk *one* edition, the written homage another—and beyond that surely other editions of one essay—interleafing thoughts of the moment with the reading of passages of notes, designing the whole, in the case of the lecture, to take place within an hour's time.

The variety, the denseness, the suggestiveness of Whitman's thought lead me everywhere into an unwinding of themes in which the complexity from which I drew took over. His thought moves not toward conclusion and summary but toward involvement and the apprehension of the variety and copiousness of forces at work—Dante's rose and Whitman's "unseen buds."

Dante begins in such a dark thicket—"How hard a thing it is to tell what a wild, and rough, and stubborn wood this was." He means here just the actual density of his own life and of his own times. Virgil and Beatrice come to lead him out of the density of the contemporary disorder into the grand architectonic orders of the eternal as the imaginations of the Roman Empire and then of Christendom—the Empire become a Church —knew it. Avicenna, St. Thomas Aquinas, and Joachim of Fiori had furnished blueprints of the orders of the real mind and history, "goods of the intellect," which underlie Dante's poetics. But Dante had come to know, had thoroughly known, in his own lifetime, the end of all hope in the actual of just those orders which most gave his work order: pope and emperor, vicars of the orders in which the temporal and eternal are united in one reality, had profoundly betrayed that unity; and, for Dante, the temporal, the actual, was left a dark thicket, a disunity between the ideal and the real. Only in the Other World, the Hell and Heaven of the Imagination, can the architecture of that Reality in which the Ideal is embodied be raised. Dante was writing the monumental memorial of a perished hope, the mausoleum of Christendom, even as Shakespeare was to write the mausoleum of Renaissance man, of the magician or Prince.

Whitman did not believe he came at the end of a civilization but at the beginning, even, before the beginning, at the apprehension of what was yet to come. He does not represent his time but announces its coming. "America," for Whitman, is yet to come. And this theme of what America is, of what democracy is, of what the sexual reality is, of what the Self is, arises from an urgency in the conception of the Universe itself, not a blueprint but an evolution of spirit in terms of variety and a thicket of potentialities. His own work in poetry he sees so, moved by generative urgencies toward the fulfillment of a multitude of latent possibilities. And so we are actually in the throes, the throes in which the ideal and the reality are at work—now that's something to lecture from, to talk from, not recollections in tranquility, nor summations of study, but, to be in the throes of a poetry in which the poet seeks to keep alive as a generative possibility a force and intent hidden in the very beginning of things, long before the beginning of the poem, the *Leaves of Grass* having its form not, as the *Divinia Commedia* had, as the paradigm of an existing eternal form, but as the ever flowing, ever Self-creative ground of a process in which forces of awareness, Self-awareness, of declaration and of longing work and rework in the evolution of what they are, the evolution of a creative intention that moves not toward the satisfaction of some prescribed form but towards the fulfillment of a multiude of possibilities out of its seed. Whitman begins to see as we do, the flow of some prescribed form but toward the fulfillment of a multitude of as a field of being, not toward progress and improvement but toward variety and awareness of variety. The good of the earth and the sun? "There are millions of suns left."

> There was never any more inception than there is now,
> Nor any more youth or age than there is now;
> And will never be any more perfection than there is now,
> Nor any more heaven or hell than there is now.

The very wild and rough and stubborn wood which Virgil rescues Dante from—the matter of the poet's person and his world—Whitman determines to be the poet of. Taking his Self and his Law, Poetics and Politics, not in the architecture of an Other World, but in an identification with the creative forces working within masses and populations, the poet was to work toward the Wedding of the Ideal and the Actual, even as Blake had proposed a poetic marriage of Heaven and Hell in the Actual. Whitman saw within the actuality of These States the idea of an America latent and at work. Not a poetry commemorative of an established order or a poetry striving to perfect an order out of chaos, but a poetry creative "in the region of imaginative, spinal and essential attributes, something equivalent to creation . . . imperatively demanded."

In this the work of the new literature was Democracy itself at work. It was not the democracy that had appeared in the days of Adams and Jefferson; it was not a democracy that had appeared in Whitman's youth or after the Civil War. Intimations were everywhere; but there were intimations too of "the appalling dangers of universal suffrage in the United States." It was not a democracy which had appeared by the end of his life. The potentiality was there, but it involved, not only generation, but "the need, a long period to come, of a fusion of the States into the only reliable identity, the moral and artistic one"—it involved a radiational force in which a mutation of spirit would take place: "the fervid and tremendous IDEA, melting everything else with resistless heat, and solving all lesser and definite distinctions in vast, indefinite, spiritual, emotional power."

Democracy Whitman saw at work in the whole of evolution. In his old age he was to recognize a companion in Darwin, but he found himself closest to Hegel. In his homage to Carlyle, Whitman calls upon the Hegelian vision as an anchor for steadying the Carlylean ship:

> According to Hegel the whole earth, (an old nucleus-thought, as in the Vedas, and no doubt before, but never hitherto brought so absolutely to the front, fully surcharged with modern scientism and facts, and made the sole entrance to each and all,) with its infinite variety, the past, the surroundings of to-day, or what may happen in the future, the contrarieties of material with spiritual, and of natural with artificial, are all, to the eye of the *ensemblist,* but necessary sides and unfoldings, different steps or links, in the endless process of Creative thought, which, amid numberless apparent failures and contradictions, is held together by central and never-broken unity—not contradictions or failures at all, but radiations of one consistent and eternal purpose. . . .

Democracy was the politics of the ensemble, as Hegel's was the philosophy of the ensemble, and Whitman saw his *Leaves of Grass* as belonging to the poetics of the ensemblist. The word "ensemblist" he italicizes. Dreaming of the ensemble of created and creating forms, Whitman was the poet of primary intuitions, ancestor of Whitehead's *Process and Reality* and of our own vision of creation where now we see all of life as unfoldings, the revelations of a field of potentialities and latencies toward species and individuals hidden in the DNA, a field of generations larger than our humanity. Back of our own contemporary arts of the collagist, the assembler of forms, is the ancestral, protean concept, wider and deeper, of the poet as devotée of the ensemble. Back of the field as it appears is Olson's proposition of composition by field is the concept of the cosmos as a field of fields. Our field in which we see the form of the poem happening belongs ultimately to, is an immediate apprehension of or sense of locality in "the infinite variety, the past, the surroundings of to-day, or what may happen in the future," the grand ensemble Whitman evokes.

Whitman was a nineteenth-century poet and he comes on with many other attitudes and ideas that seem conventions of his day. We find him talking about progress and ideals, even in the most moving passages, in a tone of assumed moral enthusiasm that, out of tune with our own sense of proprieties, reminds us that he belongs to the Victorian age. He delights in the fact that he is a man of diversities—but, very important in this discussion where I am often swept along by Whitman's spirit and thought, he was a man of contradictions and he calls up inner contradictions in the reader. His ideals, as you will appreciate, the very ideals of the potentialities of Democracy, of "America," of "scientism," as he calls it, and of "*men* here worthy the name . . . athletes" and "a strong and sweet Female Race, a race of perfect Mothers"—they are the staunchly held core of Whitman's popular appeal—have revealed potentialities of their own in the century since *Leaves of Grass* and *Democratic Vistas.* The truth of forces "a long time to come," of creative change distributed over vast populations and periods of time and written in microscopic terms out of a great variation of individual types, is one truth of the ideal: the forcing of an ideal in any immediate event will be untrue. In the late nineteen-thirties, as I came into some kind of social consciousness, ideas of Whitman's had come also to be the ideas of established and increasingly coercive governments. Totalism—*ensemblism*—is haunted when we return to it today in the dark monstrosities of socialistic and democratic totalitarianism.

Is it the deadly boast of the Chauvinist, the patriotic zeal of a spiritual imperialism, that fires Whitman's: "The Americans of all nations at any time upon the earth have probably the fullest poetical nature. The United States themselves are essentially the greatest poem"? Presidents, congresses, armed forces, industrialists, governors, police forces, have rendered the meaning of "America" and "the United States" so fearful—causing fear and filled with fear—in our time that no nationalistic inspiration comes innocent of the greed and ruthless extension of power to exploit the peoples and natural resources of the world that has spread terror, misery, and devastation wherever it has gone.

Yet, reading these passages of the 1855 Preface, stronger than the contradiction, the mysterious message comes through, translating and transforming meanings. It comes as one of the great prophecies of the nature of our American experience. Yes, all that we would most disown remains, and unless we do come to change the meaning of "nation," of "state," of "America," of "at any time upon the earth," so that these are terms of "the fullest poetical nature," we must disown. What, in the light of "the fullest poetical nature" does Whitman mean by "America"?

> The American poets are to enclose old and new for America is the race of races . . . the expression of the American poet is to be transcendant and new. It is to be indirect and not direct or descriptive or epic. Its quality goes through these to much more. Let the age and wars of other nations be chanted, and their eras and characters be illustrated and that finish the verse. Not so the great psalm of the republic. Here the theme is creative and has vista.

It was the nation of nations, the race composed of all races. It was the first time that out of no time and no where, yet out of every time then and every where, a nation had appeared. The United States of Adams and Jefferson saw itself as a mixture of European peoples, yes, but predominantly an extension of English dreams on a new continent. But in Whitman's time—it is the crux of the Civil War—the slave was freed, admitted into the community of the free, potentially the spiritual son of those who had proclaimed a Land of the Free and brother of those who continued that faith; Africa was admitted along with Europe into the unity, the "one nation." In the course of the nineteenth-century immigration, it became apparent that all the peoples of the world were represented in this one people. The nation of many nations, "the race of races"—no other country in the world has so many of the peoples of the world among its citizens.

Writing the poem "The Soldiers," I came to read Whitman's lines *"The United States themselves are essentially the greatest poem"* and *"The Americans of all nations at any time upon the earth"* in a new inspiration. Whitman's genius here is oracular. Prophetic. The oracular mode enters poetry and history where profound contradictions come into play. In the widening of what we call the credibility gap, incredible transformations may come into the statement of the truth. Oracles are to be read many ways or both ways. And here, where "the greatest poem" underlies all, the "United States" appeared to me as the states of being or of Man united, all one's states of mind brought together in one governance; and "the Americans of all nations at any time upon the earth" meant clearly that "America" and being "American" was a community that was from the beginning of Man and everywhere in the world. You could tell them by just those virtues of free men that Whitman extols: the free, creative individualist, having and keeping his own inner lawfulness, and the concern for the good of his community—mankind his people —in which that lawfulness has its ground. Is it from Vanzetti's letters or from Whitman's thought?—it will be from both and others too that the lines came to me in writing *The Multiversity:*

> Where there is no commune,
>   the individual volition has no ground.
> Where there is no individual freedom, the commune
>   is falsified.

And again:

> There being no common good, no commune,
> no communion, outside the freedom of
>   individual volition.

Once we read the United States as belonging to the greatest poem, the race of all races, and we hear Whitman speaking of Americans through-out the population of Man—every place and any place and time of Man —then, underlying these United States and this America, comes a mystery of "America" that belongs to dream and desire and the reawakening of earliest oneness with all peoples—at last, the nation of Mankind at large. It is this that informs Whitman's enthusiasm for America. In the language of Poetry, of "the greatest poem," we rightly read him in the light of Blake's visions of America, direful as they are, the States are seen by the poet as states of Man, and what is happening in the Revolution happens, in Blake's world, not because the colonies are English but because they are colonies of Man. The drama he reads in his figures of fire and outrage and imprisonment and volcanic release is a drama "of all nations at any time upon the earth."

Whitman's politics, like Dante's, is the politics of a polis that is a poem. In both the Preface of 1855 and *Democratic Vistas* Whitman insists that the heart or soul of this matter of America and of democracy is poetic. He comes not to bring a new religion but to bring—more faith-ful to the truth of things than religion—a poetry. "The time straying toward infidelity and confections and persiflage he withholds by steady faith," Whitman says of the poet in the Preface. "Faith is the antiseptic of the soul—it pervades the common people and preserves them—they never give up believing and expecting and trusting." In the pathos of this resolution, these are the people of a poetry. It is a poetic faith that informs them, a poem, not a nation, they have in common. It is the poet of *Leaves of Grass*, faithful to his mission there, and his readers, faithful followers of the text, and I among them, who "never give up believing and expecting and trusting."

Dante in his *De Monarchia*, seeking the legitimacy of government and the definition of Man's good, finds that the legitimacy of government must lie in "the ultimate goal of human civilization as a whole," in a "civilization of civilizations"—is this not Whitman's "greatest poem"? And he finds that the ultimate goal implies "some function proper to humanity as a whole for which that same totality of men is ordained in so great a multitude, to which function neither one man nor one family, nor one district nor one city-state, nor any individual kingdom may attain." May this not be Whitman's "democracy," a people resonant with the poetry of their common intent? The goal or good of the people, Dante argues, is the fulfillment of their humanity. "The specific potentiality of humanity as such is a potentiality or capacity of intellect"—we would remember here Virgil's words to Dante at Hell-gate: "We are come to the place where I told thee thou shouldst see the wretched people, who have lost the good of the intellect"; and, further, this good of the intellect lies in the *ensemble*—it is, we feel, the individual's imagination of the good of the whole population of man. "And since that same potentiality cannot all be reduced to actuality at the same time by one man, or by any of the limited associations distinguished above," Dante continues, "there must needs be multiplicity in the human race, in order for the whole of this potentiality to be actualized thereby." Dante imagines the Empire of One Spirit, a Princedom extending over and preserving the peace and guaranteeing the fulfillment of all beings and things, each free at last, that is, dwelling in the law of its own nature. "Like as there must be a multiplicity of things generable in order that the whole potentiality of first matter may always be in act. . . ."

The monarchy in Dante's *De Monarchia* proves to rest in a mystery, the rule of a Christ-spirit, beyond Christendom, in one Prince who can only be identical with the intent hidden in the true nature of each individual man if he be free to follow his own inner law, the Christ within. The tradition—it is the tradition of a poetry—continues in Whitman's insistence on the poet, the first member of the democratic possibility, as "seer . . . individual . . . complete in himself . . . the president of regulation. . . ." Law is hidden in us, for it—our share of the Law—is what we must create as we create our selves. To be individual is to recognize one's nature, or the Nature in one, to be conscious and conscientious in thought and action. On one hand:

> Whatever comprehends less than that . . . whatever is less than the laws of light and of astronomical motion . . . or less than the laws that follow the thief the liar the glutton and the drunkard through this life and doubtless afterward . . . or less than vast stretches of time or the slow formation of density or the patient upheaving of strata—is of no account.

Self is most intensely experienced in the individual's unique identity as part of the universe at large where the truth of law must comprehend whatever he is to be. Whitman draws upon Lyell in 1855, before Darwin, and before Hegel comes upon his horizon. The logic of earth and of an emerging concept of the physical universe shifts the meaning and imagination of individualities and masses; laws are not imposed upon things, but flowing from things; laws are not of imposed orders but of emerging orders. Today, in the vast democracy in which the events of particles replace the hierarchies of the atomic elements as the creative ground, Whitman's concept of the individual and the mass gains in reality. "These understand the law of perfection in masses and floods . . . that it is profuse and impartial . . . that there is not a minute of the light or dark nor an acre of the earth or sea without it." This idea of the law as a creative entity, creating itself, fires Whitman's imagination wherever he touches upon it.

> He sees health for himself in being one of the mass . . . . he sees the hiatus in singular eminence. To the perfect shape comes common ground. To be under the general law is great for that is to correspond with it.

In all, the very nature of the mass is flowered forth in individualities, new events force new comprehensions of the law. The inner lawfulness of the individual is that he is himself a term of what law is, the critic, the crisis, in the law at large. "The law of laws," Whitman calls it: "the law of successions." What we feel lawful tests the law as it tests our lives.

In *Democratic Vistas* he sees the creative life of politics as a dialectic process in which two forces play: Democracy, "the leveler, the unyielding principle of the average," and "another principle, equally unyielding. .... the counterpart and offset whereby Nature restrains the deadly original relentlessness of all her first-class laws"—"the individuality, the pride and centripetal isolation of a human being in himself—identity—personalism." Where Dante had written "Intellect" as the potentiality of humanity, Whitman writes "Personality." For both, Intellect and Personality demanded the largest population of human possibilities for its fulfillment; only in the ensemble could they take the ground of ultimate loyalties.

Dante's vision had itself drawn upon the Islamic world outside the European and even the Christian bounds. His Beatrice, the moving spirit of his vision, rimes with a power, angelic and female, the Active Intellect, who belongs to the Sufi revelation. Truth was gathered beyond the bounds of Christendom in the very world of Islam that Christian orthodoxy held most to be the Enemy, as today the dominant orthodoxy of these States holds the Communist world to be the Enemy. For those of us who are *ensemblists* and hold in faith that the Truth of Man is to be found in the resonances of the totality, the truth of democracy lies beyond the bounds of democracy; the truth of "America" is larger, if it be true, than the confines of this nation. Whitman too had come into contact with a world beyond that of Western thought; there had been a passage *from* India as well as the passage to India. The Vedas stood in his mind as part of the greatest poem to which his *Leaves* belonged.

We are in the throes of such an expansion of the imagination in time and space beyond the confines of established policies; a politics beyond cities and nations and civilizations claims our loyalties. For those of us who believe in the unity of mankind, in a new anthropology that no longer thinks of different stages of man, of a progress from primitive to civilized but in terms of different ways of being man; for those of us who further believe in the unity of living beings, the very word "humanity" extends beyond our species to involve us in a largest democracy, in an allegiance to an ecological order: the humanity of man, the difference between the population unaware—the mobocracy—and the population aware of what humanity means—the democracy—extends as far and deep in meaning as his understanding of his relation to his world extends. What we envision as being the well-being of Nature becomes the condition of our humanity. It will never—when will it be settled?

We are, here in the United States of America, the one place where all the peoples of the world are at last gathered together, and we are experiencing what? Of course, we have all the upthroes continually that the world has; old wars between peoples become wars within this one people. The common intent, the contradictions, the world-wide dissensions brought together. Not one religion, but many religions—something larger than religion is needed. Not one race, but many races—something larger than race is needed. America, the melting pot of the world, we saw it as in the thirties. The old orders of races, of ethnic groups, of languages, of religions, of classes to be broken up and mixed, interacting.

Right here in one country. Russia extends between Europe and Asia with many peoples, but they remain ethnically distinct. A visitor from Yugoslavia sees our racial troubles as a symptom of disorder: "We have five races in Yugoslavia," he told me, "and they have learned to live in harmony; they speak their own languages and live in their own parts of the country." He implies that we Americans suffer from some lack of courtesy. Order consists in keeping differences of class and race in order, never speaking out of order or moving into what is not one's place. I said, "I don't think you understand what the term means here." What can they understand where ethnic and even family differences are still thought to be the terms of some individuality? What is at issue in the development of free individuals, men whose identity moves beyond their own origins, beyond race, beyond tribe, beyond class?

Well, let me start here with a passage from my notebooks written along a line that setting out as a path was, as other attempts were, deserted in the field of apprehensions that Whitman's verse called up. "*Who learns my lesson complete?*" the passage from *Leaves of Grass* begins. So, the promise of an incompleteness led me on in the first place. So many extensions of meaning set my own meanings into motion from themselves, out into the promise of a field of rank growth beyond the projects of city-planning and coordinations, beyond the suburbs, that describe the limits of orderly discourse. The country road rambles and woods take over. In itself this is an experience of Whitman to relate, the multiphasic suggestion of his poetry. He demands ever fresh beginnings, and discountenances conclusions. I called his mode oracular. He himself again and again speaks of the copious, the seminal, the pervasive. He seeks a poetry that will convey his experience of a life that is profusely creative of meanings and in that profusion ever coming forward with diverse hints and potentialities.

We have inherited from Whitman or from our common American spirit an urge that seeks to scatter itself abroad, to send rootlets out into a variety of resources in deriving itself. "No, let me cast aside what begins to take shape and start exploring him afresh," the thought comes ever into the words as I have been writing toward this essay. "Let me start a wandering talk that may come upon some new angle." So, in my talk I did wander from my previous material, and found my concern forming itself along the line of ideas of law and of order in Poetry and the Universe. Just here, my thought returns to the passage from *Leaves of Grass*, from one of the eleven poems which follow "Song of Myself" in the 1855 edition, with which I had thought at first to begin:

> Who learns my lesson complete?
> Boss and journeyman and apprentice? . . . . churchman and atheist?
> The stupid and the wise thinker . . . . parents and offspring. . . .
>   merchant and clerk and porter and customer . . . . editor,
>   author, artist and schoolboy?
>
> Draw nigh and commence,
> It is no lesson . . . . it lets down the bars to a good lesson,
> And then to another . . . . and every one to another still.
>
> The great laws take and effuse without argument,
> I am of the same style, for I am their friend. . . .

As always with Whitman, we will find back of the inspired and enthusiastic phrases the information of a perennial study; his resonances have knowledgeable roots in the ground of the evolution of ideas. The lesson of science in the nineteenth century, in the geology of Lyell, in the biology of Darwin, as in the concept of history after Hegel, was that science was ever to be fruitfully incomplete; and here Whitman proposed a poetry that would be the companion of science. Truth, the grass, was for him the matter of generations, of roots and seedings, in which primary intuitions of the universe are at work to realize themselves.

Back of this Friend of the Great Laws, writing in the same style he saw Life at work in, in the evolution of the poet of *Leaves of Grass*, rightly the name *Friend* will recall Whitman's own Quaker origins and the advent of "the Society of Friends" in America. And we may trace this concept of *Friend* back along the way it has traveled in the evolution of identities from the mystical experience and testimony of George Fox to those Friends of God and the Friends of the Free Spirit, who in the late Middle Ages were Adamites—returning to the conditions of Eden, bearded and naked. We will find there the genetic origins in a Christian tradition of Whitman's recurring themes of nakedness and beardedness; and, today, about us, a century after Whitman, we will recognize his spiritual kin among the new generation of Adamites.

In his essay "George Fox (and Shakespeare.)," Whitman sees Shakespeare as "born and bred of similar stock, in much the same surroundings and station in life—from the same England—and at a similar period. . . . fancy's lord, imagination's heir," Shakespeare radiating "a splendor so dazzling that he himself is almost lost in it"—is, indeed, lost in it, for in the dialectics of history, in the development of new spiritual species, it is George Fox who, for Whitman, embodies "something too—a thought— the thought that wakes in silent hours—perhaps the deepest, most eternal thought latent in the human soul." Shakespeare has the splendor of manifest themes that incarnate in its swan-song an historical species—Whitman sees it as the Feudal order. Greatness like that of the Greek dramatists, of Dante, of Shakespeare, can be seen to belong not to the growth and life of the orders they spring from but to the terminal stage. The richness of Shakespeare, "all literature's splendor," "made for the divertisement only of the élite of the castle, and from its point of view," "his infinitely royal, multiform quality"—belongs to an extinct order of life that grows enormous in the period of its extinction, as reptiles at the end of the Age of Reptiles grew into such dragons as have haunted the poetic imagination of Man from his earliest times. "When Feudalism, like a sunset, seem'd to gather all its glories, reminiscences, personalisms, in one last gorgeous effort, before the advance of a new day, a new incipient genius. . . ." The generative orders lie in the common man; it is George Fox who will be the spiritual progenitor of the *Leaves of Grass*. But *Leaves of Grass* in turn is an event in Poetry which today we see, as Whitman saw Shakespeare gathering the glory of Feudalism, gathering the grand sweep of a Democracy, an expanding nationalism, into a great sun that casts its splendors long after its time has past. For surely, no less than Shakespeare's kings and commons and his courtly lovers, Whitman's heroic workers and comrades in love, strong in their individual selves, come to our minds as grandeurs out of perished worlds. Like dragons, they have entered the generative stuff of our humanity.

Back of his coupling of Shakespeare and George Fox in the essay on Fox—"one to radiate all of art's, all literature's splendor" and the other to carry into the community a spiritual latency, yet both "born and bred of similar stock, in much the same surroundings and station in life"—is a genetic drama of alternate potentialities within one nature. Shakespeare in fulfilling his individual genius rises to eminence from the mass; specializing, he is beyond reproduction. The poetic genius too, like the genius of law, works in successions. All grand realizations but clear the way of the urgency toward reality that was all theirs. The achieved is that which is removed from the field of generation or quest of achievement.

"Poetry, largely consider'd, is an evolution," Whitman writes in "*A Thought on Shakspere*": "sending out improved and ever-expanded types —in one sense, the past, even the best of it, necessarily giving place, and dying out. For our existing world, the bases on which all the grand old poems were built have become vacuums. . . ." *Leaves of Grass* and its poet, the grandly conceived personality Whitman created, are designed "to radiate all of art's, all literature's splendor." But, "born and bred of similar stock, in much the same surroundings," there might be another genius in the work. Within *Leaves of Grass*, more important than its splendors, a seed "latent in the human soul." From the same mass Shakespeare raises the word to an individualized splendor; George Fox returns the word to the anonymity of the mass, to its silent commonality. And readers of *Leaves of Grass* will not only—it is Whitman's dream—find in it the masterpiece that makes Whitman kingly among democrats, but will find in it a common testimony. In the essay on Fox, Whitman might be speaking of this second poet of *Leaves:* "Thus going on, there is something in him that fascinates one or two here, and three or four there, until gradually there were others who went about in the same spirit, and by degrees the Society of Friends too shape, and stood among the thousand religious sects of the world. Women also catch the contagion, and go round, often shamefully misused." Behind these figures of a courageous religious sect to. which Whitman's ancestors belonged, we see the figures of the little company who became a Society of Friends for *Leaves of Grass.*

That "deepest most eternal thought latent in the human soul" which George Fox embodies—"that waits in silent hours"—is the seed of a generative silence behind the Word, the seed of latency or intent that informs the ensemble. The ultimate depth belongs, for Whitman, to the revelation of the latent, and the ultimate revelation lies beyond our powers and yet within all powers. It cannot be "realized" by us for we belong to the process of such realization, it does not belong to us. Whitman is always, then, a compound in his conception, companion of Shakespeare in his grand poetic projection, and companion of Fox, the convert of a mystical experience in poetry. Out of the laws of succession in Poetry, out of the temporal excitement of "improved and ever-expanded types" at work in one, comes a call to Poetry, a call to Order, a call to bear Eternal Witness. The poet then like George Fox must set out to work by faith, beyond belief and beneath contempt.

Setting out in 1855, Whitman had to go on faith. He had the courage of a grand fidelity. But he had no alternative. The poem commanded him. Its reality and truth were imperative. It commands me reading today—the vision of what the Poem is, and within that, *Leaves of Grass* as it has been for me in my own creative life an incarnation of that Presence of a Poetry. This body of words the medium of this spirit. Writing or reading, where words pass into this commanding music, I found a presence of person more commandingly real than what I thought to be my person before; Whitman or Shakespeare presenting more of what I was than I was. And in the course of my own poetry what has drawn me into its depths is this experience of a more intense presence of world and self than I know in myself.

We are just emerging from a period that was long dominated by the idea of a poem as a discipline and a form into which the poet put ideas and feelings, confining them in a literary propriety, giving them the bounds of sound and sense, rime and reason, and the values of a literary—a social—sensibility. Poetry was to be brought to heel, obedient to the criteria of rational discourse, of social realities, of taste. For the New Criticism of the 1930s and 1940s, it was most important that the poet not put on airs. The dominant school of that time thought of form not as a mystery but as a manner of containing ideas and feelings; of content not as the meaning of form but as a commodity packaged in form. It was the grand age of Container Design; and critics became consumer researchers, wary of pretentious claims and seeking solid values. Ideas were thought of as products on the market.

But Whitman's ideas flow as his work flows. He knows that thought is a melody and not something that you manufacture. Poetic thought, Carlyle had proposed, was *musical* thought. And Whitman's verse, as has been amply studied, has form as an aria has form, a pouring forth of thought, not a progression but a medium of thought. The presence belongs to the mass. His imagination of the form at issue, his poetics, moves out from the potentiality he recognized in the aria of the solo singer toward a concept of form to come, of meanings to come. "It poured like a raging river more than any thing else I could compare it to," he writes to a young man in the hospital in Washington in 1863 of an operatic voice: "it is like a miracle—no mocking bird nor the clearest flute can begin with it." But it is a mocking bird or thrush, "solitary, singing in the West," that begins with it for Whitman; and it may be, as it was too in ancient times, poetry began in the music of a flute playing—the forms and meanings that began to flow along the line of another melody. Bird-sound or flute-sound, and words over-heard in their melody by the enraptured ear. That raging river of sound, the aria, becomes in the vision of Whitman a song of the sea, and ever within it, and contrasting, the solitary bird-song of the individual to the Beloved. So too, he found inspiration in throngs—the currents of Broadway within the sea of Manhattan, the throngs upon the ferry boats. The other day, waiting on the steps of the New York Public Library, I found myself giving myself over to contemplate the crowd in the spirit of Whitman, looking at the individual people going about their ways, not watching the individual, but in all, watching the mass of them. Throngs, much as we know the dreadful approaching and already erupting consequences of the swarming and ever-breeding population freed of the information of disease and death, still convey the sense of an exhiliration. There is a thrill about the potentialities of masses of people. So many lives, one feels.

Even the thrill of. . . . Well, there was the thrill of all those people walking in that area, of a complicated choreography, unconscious, multi-phasic accommodations made to the presences moving each along its own conscious way. It was a fine day, however, and the noon-time mood responded to the sunlight and the Spring tide. But even the thrill that whatever we fear out of this monstrous growth of population the future is at work there. This little ensemble and beyond it, the very present, vast ensemble of the City itself—its millions beyond one's comprehension but ever commanding one's apprehensions—calling up for a moment the thrill of the grand ensemble it belongs to.

The element of depth belongs, to Whitman, it has seemed to me, to the revelation of the ensemble in which time moves not toward the end of things but to the fulfillment of things. But now it seems, that word "fulfillment" has too much of the Biblical idea of things fulfilled in the Apocalypse. How far from Whitman's sense of what it means, of filling and fullness, my own poetic apocalyptic sense of signs and meanings fulfilled is. And much has been made of Whitman's alliance with the Vedas, with that endlessness and fullness. And I grow impatient with Whitman's theme of improvement and progress, until I see that theme as one of grander vistas, coming not to the End but into the Full Sea of Time. The crowds upon the Manhattan streets, the throngs of living beings we apprehend, enlarge vividly the impact of "the commonalty of all humanity, all time," in which Whitman in his essay on Darwinism sees that the poet "must indeed recast the old metal, the already achiev'd material, into and through new moulds, current forms."

"Who learns my lesson complete?" Nature asks, who learns my lesson complete? History asks, who learns my lesson complete? The Creative Self at work in Creation toward the realization of Self asks, who learns my lesson complete? *Leaves of Grass* was itself a lesson not to be learned complete. The poet returned to his work there in edition after edition. Not addition after addition, but furnishing forth each time a life of the book. What leaf completes the leaves? Each leaf in the ensemble an act of completion. The ensemble, alone the field of the complete, haunts the work of the artist who makes in the poem a fiction of the existence of the whole, a fictional ensemble in which we become aware of the ensemble.

Whitman opens up, beyond Nature and History, an intent and drama of God as Creator at work in the Ensemble to realize his Creative Self. When Whitman thinks of the tradition his vision belongs to, he does not list Heraclitus, but here he is most Heraclitean, for the followers of Heraclitus were most accused of just this heresy, that they believed in a Universe in the process of Its Self-realization. This God does not learn His Self—his lesson—complete except in the totality of Creation, for his learning and his creating are one. The grand Maker or Poet makes his Self come real—realizes Himself—as he makes the field of the Real. We learn who we are by living—we are ourselves the mass of our individualities. Lesson undoes lesson.

"Draw nigh and commence," Whitman continues. Then let's take the contradiction the oracle proposes *"It is no lesson—it lets down the bars to a good lesson, /* And that to another, and every one to another still." Hidden in this passage of learning and that in turn a freedom opening upon another learning is the relation of the individual unique undertaking of here and now and the *En Masse.*

God is boss, journeyman, and apprentice, of His own Work, as Whitman, in turn, as poet, creator, is boss, journeyman and apprentice. Did the editions of 1855, 1860, 1871, 1889, 1891 represent a progress toward completion for him? Or an everlasting command to draw nigh and commence, revealing in the old metal, the already achiev'd material, new demands? As we begin to see evolution as a field in which series of variations, visions and revisions, and mutations, impulses and inspirations anew, are at work, these Leaves of Grass are individual reincarnations of a single identity. For my parents, who were theosophical in their religion, Whitman's recurring hints of reincarnation belief were read straight across the board, were taken as the lesson. But draw nigh and commence, the poet asked. This lesson but lets down the bars to another possibility. We see in the course of Whitman's life and works a law of successions, fully achieved versions of *Leaves of Grass* that prove to be given over into the new life of yet another edition.

The line of individual consciousness, of "draw nigh and commence," is the line of an ever-breaking of a wave upon the shore of its sea. Recalling in the close of this essay, the solo of the bird rising in the choral song of the sea, let us, for the moment, take the melody of the bird as identical with the hovering line of the surf-wave, ever about to break, ever drawing nigh and commencing. This configuration I see writing itself again and again in the terms that move through Whitman's work—the word "En-Masse," that war, that Whitman tells the Muse of War his poetry wages:

> . . . a longer and greater one than any,
> Waged in my book with varying fortune, with flight, advance
> and retreat, victory deferr'd and wavering,
> . . . . . the field the world . . .

at one with the Sea, the all encompassing "I"; at one with the bird, lonely, isolate; and, song of the bird heard mingled and commingling with the surf, the self and the Over-Self at one in the breaking line of the wave seen. The informing figure is here.

What philosophies, but particularly here rationalist philosophy and those philosophers of higher mind who would free thought and identity from the bonds of the sensual, the imaginative, and the passionate, relegate to the realm of illusions and ephemera—the illustrational immediacies of color and sound—are for the artist the deepest ground of the real. In the poem, the voice given at last its aria, the living pulse and indwelling resonances, is the true body; and the Incarnation of the Word is all, that It is embodied in the sound is all, and sound in the stations of a melody or passionate sequence. The sound incarnates and informs. In this theology, the Word is identical with its body, having its life in the interrelating vowels and consonants in which its voice comes. The center of this reality is what seems the most evanescent of sensual facts, the life of a man as the center of a universe, the duration of a tone as the center of a music, the configuration of sea and the singer as the center of consciousness moving outward.

"*I sing*," rings out in the opening Inscription of the *Leaves* in the 1871 edition: "One's-Self I Sing." This is the orphic poet, at one with the bird outpouring its orizons.

> . . . at dawn the unrivall'd one, the hermit thrush from the swamp-
>   cedars,
> Solitary, singing in the West, I strike up for a New World.

And at one too with the sea:

> . . . the long pulsation, ebb and flow of endless motion,
> The tones of unseen mystery, the vague and vast suggestions
>   of the briny world, the liquid-flowing syllables. . . .

"*This is the ocean's poem*," he declares in the third inscription of the 1881 edition. "*In Cabin'd Ships at Sea*," the "ship," his book to be, at once "*sailing athwart the imperious waves*" and an extension of the deep itself, for these waves are the imperious lines of the verse. The poem is vehicle and actuality of the wave of feeling it rides. "*Chant on, sail on*," the poet commands; but this chanting that is also a sailing is the wave itself of the sea it sails upon.

In the poem "Eidólons" of 1876, the substance "*Of every human* life/ (The units gather'd, posted, not a thought, emotion, deed, left out,)"

> Ever the ateliers, the factories divine,
>   Issuing eidólons

is the surf of a sea upon some shore:

> Ever the dim beginning,
> Ever the growth, the rounding of the circle,
> Ever the summit and the merge at last, (to surely start again,)
>   Eidólons! eidólons!

> Ever the mutable,
> Ever materials, changing, crumbling, re-cohering. . . .

at once the very kinetics of Whitman's own line structure within the poem, of poem structure within the *Leaves of Grass*, of edition upon edition of that book, and of his sense of the essential informing motion of the life of Man and of the Universe:

> All space, all time,
> (The stars, the terrible perturbation of the suns,
> Swelling, collapsing, ending, serving their longer, shorter use,) . . .

Here, in Whitman's physics, the vision of the cosmos in process appears as a Sea, and the individual personal Sun, the center of creation for Earth's parochial perspectives and the prototype of God as Father and King, is, in this perspective of "all space, all time," the ensemble, given over to a higher reality of the terrible perturbation of suns, a star now among the throngs of stars, no longer the paradigm of laws but serving a "longer, shorter use" in a source of laws beyond paradigm. Space, time, and the sea of stars, as well as the sea of men to which the individuality of man belongs, as well as the form of the chant arising in language—these are expressions of a Sea, a Sea that is itself both cradle and babe, "endlessly rocking," "swelling, collapsing."

To our post-Freudian reading, the bird pouring forth its passionate song from its leafy convert and the poet's "chant of dilation or pride" betray a sexual configuration, and the "word out of the sea" will be, as it was for Whitman,

> Out of the boy's mother's womb, and from the nipples of her
>   breasts,
> Out of the Ninth Month midnight . . .

In the later version, "Out of the Cradle Endlessly Rocking," the direct image of the boy's mother, womb and nipples, is removed (and yet insistent enough to intrude at the close of the poem, a line not there in the earlier "Reminiscence": "(Or like some old crone rocking the cradle, swathed in sweet garments, bending aside,)" but the Sea remains "with angry moans the fierce old mother incessantly moaning." Yet we might go further in our Freudian reading to see that for the poet the genital reality and the infantile sexuality evoked in the womb and nipples are not the primary content but lead to the primary content. We might follow here the Freudian disciple Sandor Ferenczi in *Thalassa* where he proposes that "the mother would, properly, be the symbol of and partial substitute for the sea, and not the other way about." Yes, the cradle imitates and restores by man's invention the rocking of the embryo in the amniotic fluid, but the amniotic fluid in turn recapitulates in the land-mammal the warmth and surging of the primal Sea in which the seeds of Life first quickened, the male and female discharging their seed-cells, spermatazoa and eggs, into the oceanic medium in a pre-genital sexuality. "The amniotic fluid," Ferenczi suggests, "represents a sea 'introjected,' as it were, into the womb of the mother."

Our reading of the poet then may follow our reading of the psycho-analyst to see in the ecstasy of the orgasm a return into present feeling, into consciousness, of the origins, the return of a life (as in death one may be supposed to recall all of life) going back beyond the boundaries of the individual, beyond the boundaries of species, to the Primal Scene of Creation—the Sea of the Universe in which suns pour forth, live and die. The more appropriately in that Whitman had been a forerunner of Freud in this conviction that the whole question of sexuality "strikes far, very far deeper than most people have supposed." "Is it not really an intuition of the human race?" he asks in *A Memorandum at a Venture*, seeing in our sexual consciousness, as in democratic vistas, not something concluded but the promise of something yet to come, an apprehension in the present: "For, old as the world is, and beyond statement as are the countless and splendid results of its culture and evolution, perhaps the best and earliest and purest intuitions of the human race have yet to be develop'd."

The sexual theme is ever-present then as an intuition of the cosmos at large, as in turn the actual bird and the actual sea, once experienced in boyhood, returned to, is an intuition that opens into the feeling of being with a poetry beyond poetry "old as the world is." When, for the poet, the aria "convulses me like the climax of my love-grip," we are not mistaken to recognize in the bird's song pouring forth the pouring forth of semen in orgasmic release. But simile for Whitman is not a mere form of speech, it is a formula of feeling, and that feeling—it is the basis of his poetic understanding—where it arises in the course of the climax of a love-grip or of a poetic seizure, has the authenticity of a primal intuition.

"The oath of procreation I have sworn—my Adamic and fresh daughters," he declares in "Enfans d'Adam," as in the 1860 edition his identification with the Self of the universe and with Man is woven through with another identification with the Adam, male *and* female, and the bisexual ideal, haunting, as it will for the rest of his life, his actual homosexuality. The poet labors to unite the Ideal—and Whitman sees the Ideal not as belonging to the world of high-minded paradigms but to the world of primordial latencies—and the Real, even as his mission is to present a path between the Real and the individual soul. Awkwardly and pathetically, the ideal of bisexuality—not for Whitman of *being* both sexes but of having both sexes as lovers—remains inchoate. He seems not to express but to lay claim to or even boast his sexual love of women. Nowhere is there the physical longing and intensity of loss and gain in feeling that informs the love poems of male lovers. Yet it is a homosexuality in distress, not only in its cry for a mate—there are also the ardent raptures of its fulfillments—but in its generative loss. Mates must be, Whitman sees, "daughters, sons, preluding"; and in the longing for a woman not as lover but as mother to his fathering desire, the intensity of his longing rings true: "I pour the stuff to start sons and daughters fit for These States—I press with rude muscle . . ." "The greed that eats me night and day with hungry gnaw, till I saturate what shall produce boys to fill my place when I am through." But this progeny now must be progeny of his words, the throng of lives invisible in his semen and the throng of readers invisible in his words (or readings invisible in his words) identified; but seminal words never satisfied for the actual semen. In the famous reply to Symonds' enquiry concerning the *Calamus* theme, it is this claim to actual offspring that seems most urgent in answer: "I have had six children—two are dead—One living southern grandchild, fine boy, who writes to me occasionally . . ." As old agony of the heart bursts forth even in his last years.

> Urge and urge and urge,
> Always the procreant urge of the world . . .

"The song of me rising from bed and meeting the sun" pours forth in *Leaves of Grass* in a rapture and sense of plenitude that mimics the ever present sexual image, the ejaculation of semen, the jetting of a multitude in which one spermatazoa may come to the consummation of its egg, a host jetted forth to live the lifetime of each its own as a sperm. Here again we find the terrible perturbation of the suns, seeds of sons Whitman never fathered, "swelling, collapsing, ending, serving their longer, shorter use." And answering the poet's fathering disappointment, his wisdom extends its sympathetic identification beyond the actual: "You shall possess the good of the earth and sun . . . . there are millions of suns left."

"Urge and urge and urge . . ." "*Agonía, agonía, sueño, fermento y sueño . . . agonía, agonía,*" Lorca will reply, a poet who was himself obsessed with the longing of a woman to give birth, to have a child, and denied fulfillment.

So in Whitman, song is poured forth, love is poured forth, self is poured forth, as semen is jetted, in a life urgency at once triumphant and pathetic. His young friends, his comrades, as he grows older, will be no longer lovers but his boys or sons. And he will be ever aware of the life and death at work in things, the deep coinherence of Eros and Thanatos in the love-act. By the million the seeds find no receptive ground; by the millions the seeds arrive, and Man who is like grass to the beasts of the field springs ever, like grass, anew.

> The souls moving along . . . . are they invisible while the least
>   atom of the stones is visible?
> . . . .
> What living and buried speech is always vibrating here . . . .
> . . . .
> I mind them or the resonance of them. . . . I come again and again.

In the moving words "invisible," "visible," "buried," and "vibrating," "the resonance of them," we are reminded of the felt presence of Life beyond our senses—the individual spermatazoa in its life invisible to us, itself in its own life a *soul*. But now the poem speaks of "speech," "*living and buried*," and the resonance of words become *soul*." We begin then to read the poet's "*I come again and again*" with the common sexual meaning of the word *come*.

"Resonance" will give a meaning springing from our sense of the generative orders of life to those principles of music and poetry that many take to be matters of convention and prosody. In the doctrine of resonances rime and meter are no longer thought of as regularities subscribed to or regulations imposed but as Whitman in the 1855 Preface sees rhyme "that it drops the seeds of a sweeter and more luxuriant rhyme, and of uniformity that it conveys itself into its own roots in the ground out of sight."

Poetry and science are close allies for Whitman, for each is ultimately concerned with finding the universe, at once a matter of knowing and a matter of creation. The Real is what we make it out to be. In his time he saw the break-through of science as a demand for the break-through of poetics. Poetics, physics, politics, all man's serious engagements with life are realms of one Self. A new imagination of the order of the physical universe or of the biological process demands a new imagination of poetic order. So, the political realm "America" will be ultimately "the greatest poetry"; and for its work will demand: "1st, a large variety of character" and "2nd, full play for human nature to expand itself in numberless and even conflicting directions." But this is what the poem also demands; what the origin of species in evolution demands.

The song rises into its melody and pours forth from the passionate throat even as and identical with the rising into the flowing and crumbling melodic line of the breaker of the Sea and poem, line following line to re-iterate the urgency of the poem. "Form" and "content" belong to this urgency as the form and content of the wave belong to the very existence at all of the wave.

Taking these two co-inherent figures, the bird—the phoebe-bird, mockingbird, hermit thrush, shy and hidden, crying out "Death's outlet song of life," and the "mysterious ocean where the streams empty," of the 1860 "Proto-leaf"—"prophetic spirit of materials shifting and flickering around me," the lonely, isolate melodic singer pouring forth from its utter individuality and the power *en masse* of the ensemble in which he sings, yield not only poetic meanings, extensions of meaning in terms of the relations of word, phrase, poem, sequence, and the whole, of resonances throughout, but life meanings, communal meanings, political and scientific vistas. *Democratic Vistas* are vistas of new poetics and evolutionary theory. The singing bird and the surfing sea are images in the sense that Pound revived in our tradition with his *Imagist* credo of 1912: "an intellectual and emotional complex in an instant of time," that brings "that sense of sudden liberation; that sense of freedom from time limits and space limits; that sense of sudden growth, which we experience in the presence of the greatest works of art." Here, for a moment, in the period of his initial inspiration before the First World War and the esthetics of the Modernist period, Pound contributes a link in the succession from Whitman to us as followers of Pound discovering ourselves in Whitman. In "Psychology and Troubadours," published in *The Quest* in 1916, Pound will still speak in the terms of "our kinship to the vital universe" and "about us the universe of fluid force, and below us the germinal universe"; he can refer to certain creative consciousnesses as "germinal":

> Their thoughts are in them as the thought of the tree is in the seed, or in the grass, or the grass in the grain, or the blossom. And these minds are the more poetic, and they affect mind about them, and transmute it as the seed the earth. And this latter sort of mind is close on the vital universe . . .

But Pound's thought here, with its reflections of the poet of *Leaves of Grass*, does not go forward with contemporary scientific imagination to a poetic vision of the Life Process and the Universe but goes back to Ficino and the Renaissance ideas. The *Cantos* present their own dynamic life of a universalizing Mind, having, as always, the perturbation of suns; it seems to us today the *Cantos* even more than *Leaves of Grass* presenting "a large variety of character" and expanding "in numberless and even conflicting directions." To Pound's authoritarian superego, order meant the order of totalitarian ideologies and neo-Platonic hierarchies, and the creation of his poetic genius seemed to have, like the music of Bartok or of Beethoven, "the defects inherent in a record of struggle."

The generation of Pound and Williams, like the critical generation of the 1930s and 1940s, sought to "objectify" the poem, to free it from the complex associations of life and history. In the 1950s, Williams admonished us, zealously and even intolerantly, that the poem was written with words not ideas, *made* with words, as the painting was made with paints; and the artist in making a poem made a machine or structure of words, freeing language from its contaminations beyond art. Yet for us, Pound's preaching culture and Williams' preaching art belonged to just the process beyond art, the record of struggle, they thought to stand against; and in that, their thought and their work forms an antithetical phase in the process in which Whitman appears as our thesis, preparing for a synthesis that begins in their own work in its last phase. Paterson in Williams' *Paterson* is akin, indeed, to Whitman's Myself; and the very word "Cantos," setting out upon the sea and inspired and reinspired by figures of that sea, can recall the word "Chants" of Whitman's *Leaves of Grass*, as well as the Cantos of Dante's *Divina Commedia*. The grand formal courage of Whitman's Personalism in *Leaves of Grass* was to present not argument or rationalization but, as Pound declares his own purpose in writing, "one facet and then another"—an ideogram of Self, a conglomerate Image. Once I returned to Whitman, in the course of writing *The Opening of the Field* when *Leaves of Grass* was kept as a bedside book, Williams' language of objects and Pound's ideogrammatic method were transformed in the light of Whitman's hieroglyphic of the ensemble. So too, the translation-code of Freudian psychoanalysis as, after Whitman, I draw nigh and commence, is both a lesson and "is no lesson . . . it lets down the bars to a good lesson, And then to another."

In the very place where often contemporary individualism finds identity most lost, Whitman takes the ground of his identity and person: in the "particulars and details magnificently moving in vast masses." He saw Democracy not as an intellectual ideal but as an intuition of a grander and deeper reality potential in Man's evolution, beyond the awakening of philosopher-kings and poets, the awakening of the mass. The poet was not individual in his genius, for that genius was the genius of the people; the poet in his poetry an awakening in one of the poetic intent of the mass. "A bard is to be commensurate with a people . . . His spirit responds to his country's spirit." As a dream brings into our consciousness the vision and message of the unconscious mass, so the poet speaks a dream of Man to unawakened men.

As we return to Whitman as a base, we return to just such a poetic courage as the early Pound envisions in those who would "exist close on the vital universe." In Whitman there is no ambiguity about the source of *meaning*. It flows from a "Me myself" that exists in the authenticity of the universe. The poet who exists close on the vital universe then exists close on his Self. All the events of human experience come as words of the poem of poems—the confidence stays with him:

> Lilac and star and bird twined with the chant of my soul,
> There in the fragrant pines and the cedars dusk and dim.

And in the first pages of *Leaves of Grass* 1855 he had begun, he tells us, to see the natural world as a text of hieroglyphics:

A child said, What is the grass? fetching it to me with full
    hands;
How could I answer the child? . . . . I do not know what it is
    any more than he.

I guess it must be the flag of my disposition, out of hopeful
    green stuff woven.

Or I guess it is the handkerchief of the Lord,
A scented gift and remembrancer designedly dropped,
Bearing the owner's name someway in the corners, that we may
    see and remark, and say Whose?

The grass is the very language, embodying as it does the perennial
human spirit and experience, in which the book we are reading is created;
it is the green blades of words that we call Poetry because the pulse
of that sea of grass enlivens them, common as grass, and having the
mystery of the ultimately *real*, a living word, as Whitman most wanted
his own poetry to have.

Perhaps only James Joyce, in what Ezra Pound saw as his retrograde
work, *Finnegans Wake*, among contemporaries so seizes upon the revelation of the real and of the self as the revelation of the laws of the poem
itself and of its magical authority. "The handkerchief" here that the
grass is, "gift and remembrancer" that is "designedly dropped," "bearing
the owner's name someway in the corners, that we may see and remark,
and say, Whose?" may be for some readers a passing sentimental figure,
but it may also suggest the concept of creator and creation, of the poet's
signature in his own work in a dropped hint, of the idea of signatures, gift
and memory (*Mnemosyne*, the Mother of the Muses) that is akin to the
letter that in Joyce's work the Hen has scratched up in the mound of the
book, a scrap presented by the Ensemblist.

Or I guess the grass is itself a child . . . . the produced babe of
    the vegetation.

Or I guess it is a uniform hieroglyphic.
    .   .   .   .
To me the converging objects of the universe perpetually flow,
All are written to me, and I must get what the writing means.

That in the cold mad feary father Okeanos of the Sea in *Finnegan* we may have come at last to some phase of the very Sea that speaks in *Leaves of Grass* must seem far to have come indeed. Whitman would have found Joyce's loneliness morbid and his nightmare foreign to the resolution of *Leaves*, yet the poet of *Leaves of Grass* had known currents of loneliness and nightmare. In the poem "The Sleepers," *Leaves* admits such inhabitants. And if the vast populations of man and those words "America," "the United States," and "Democracy" have been rendered fearful in Joyce's lifetime by men of his generation, the Sea too darkens.

I would think myself in the very nightmare of it, yet it is Whitman's Sea that remains primary for me. At the last, evoking that Sea in "With Husky-Haughty Lips, O Sea!," a poem from *Sands at Seventy:*

> . . . a lack from all eternity in thy content,
> (Naught but the greatest struggles, wrongs, defeats, could make
>   thee greatest—no less could make thee,) . . .

Are we troubled by the threat of sentimentality in the *thy* and *thee?* George Fox had joined a community of Friends in their courage to bring back the terms of such a brotherhood in *thee* and *thou*.

> Thy lonely state—something thou ever seek'st and seek'st, yet
>   never gain'st,
> Surely some right withheld—some voice, in huge monotonous rage,
>   of freedom-lover pent,
> Some vast heart, like a planet's, chain'd and chafing in those
>   breakers,
> By lengthen'd swell, and spasm, and panting breath,
> And rhythmic rasping of thy sands and waves,
> And serpent hiss, and savage peals of laughter,
> And undertones of distant lion roar,
> (Sounding, appealing to the sky's deaf ear—but now, rapport for
>   once,
> A phantom in the night thy confidant for once,)
> The first and last confession of the globe,
> Outsurging, muttering from thy soul's abysms,
> The tale of cosmic elemental passion,
> Thou tellest to a kindred soul.

Figure 9

Figure 10

Figure 11

Figure 12

Figure 13

Figure 14

Figure 15

Figure 16

Figure 17

Figure 18

Figure 19

Figure 20

My 71st year arrives; the fifteen past months nearly all
illness or half illness — until a tolerable day (Aug. 6 1889) & con-
voy'd by Mr. B and Ed. W. I have been carriaged across to Philadelphia
(how sunny & fresh & good look'd the river, the people, the vehicles, &
Market & Arch streets!) & have sat for this photo. wh' satisfies me.

Walt Whitman

Figure 21

Figure 22

Figure 23

Figure 24

Figure 25

Figure 26

Figure 27

WALT WHITMAN, INCITING THE BIRD OF FREEDOM TO SOAR

Figure 28

CALAMUS ILLUSTRATION
1901

CALAMUS ILLUSTRATION II
1901

Figure 29

Figure 30

Figure 31

Figure 32

Gay Wilson Allen

The Iconography
of Walt Whitman

I.

"The Iconography of Walt Whitman": if my title suggests a saint or a prophet whose followers worshiped graphic and plastic images of him, this suggestion is not entirely misleading. One reason for the enormous number of surviving photographs, sketches, oil paintings, sculptures, medals, plaques, bas reliefs, and icons of Whitman in other media is that his contemporary friends and admirers did almost literally worship the man, and to some extent cults continued after his death. He was hated, too, but few antagonistic caricatures have survived—I mean, of course, in pictorial form, for we do have many bitter attacks in words, some collected and reprinted by the poet himself, as evidence of the hostility he had to overcome.

During his lifetime Whitman enjoyed the friendship of many artists who sketched, painted, and sculpted him with various degrees of success. Since his death his character and appearance have become symbols—of democratic art, of revolt against conventionalism (he has been called the first "Hippie"), of the dignity of the common man, of degeneracy in the arts, of a modern Messiah or a reincarnation of Lao-tsu, and a variety of other imaginative abstractions—with the result that scores of artists who never knew him in the flesh have created images of him based primarily on one or more of his better-known photographs. Probably thousands of people who have never read *Leaves of Grass* can identify a picture of its author. This is partly because no other American writer of the nineteenth century, with the possible exception of Mark Twain—whose face as well as his name became a trademark—was so frequently photographed as Walt Whitman. But for Whitman, more than for Twain, many people assume that they know Whitman the poet because they are familiar with some graphic image of him. For this reason it is interesting to see what images have been most widely popular, and what conceptions of Whitman they convey.

Walt Whitman was remarkably photogenic, but this is not the whole explanation for those hundreds of photographs—and I do not exaggerate the number. The abundance of these photographs, often reproduced in newspapers and magazines, has been observed and commented upon by various biographers and critics, but no one seems to have thought of their close relationship to the history of photography in this country, or speculated on the possible influence of the development of this art on the poet himself. Although I am not ready to propose the thesis that the camera gave Whitman his "identity," I do believe that both cameras and graphic artists gave him images of himself which influenced the symbolical role he struggled to develop for himself as a "poet-prophet."

The first photographic process capable of producing a satisfactory permanent image was discovered by Louis Jacques Mandé Daguerre of Paris. The French Assembly offered him a life annuity if he would make his formulas public in order that all mankind might benefit from them, and he published them on August 19, 1839. Daguerre's discovery—or invention—was at once recognized throughout Europe as one of the great technological achievements of the age.

On September 21, 1839, the steamship *British Queen* brought copies of the August 23 issue of the London *Globe*, which gave full details of Daguerre's method, and it was big news next day in the New York newspapers. Some editors feared a hoax, but the eminent painter and inventor Samuel Morse had recently returned to the City University of New York (now New York University) after visiting Daguerre, and he vouched for the authenticity of the report. Furthermore, both he and his colleague, John W. Draper, professor of chemistry, were soon able to produce daguerreotypes of their own—though an Englishman, D. W. Seager, actually made the first successful daguerreotype in the United States on September 27, 1839. Three days later the *Morning Herald* printed this comment under the caption "THE NEW ART":

> We saw the other day, in Chilton's, in Broadway, a very curious specimen of the new mode, recently invented by Daguerre in Paris, of taking on copper the exact resemblances of scenes and living objects, through the medium of the sun's rays reflected in a *camera obscura*.

The scene embraces a part of St. Paul's church, and the surrounding shrubbery and houses, with a corner of the Astor House, and for aught we know, Stetson looking out of the window, telling a joke about Davie Crockett. All this is represented on a small piece of copper equal in size to a miniature painting.

The *Herald* further reported that the camera had been directed at the subject in bright sunlight for "eight or ten minutes," then adding, "in Europe a longer exposure is required because an American sun shines brighter than the European."

At the time of this great excitement over the "new art" in the autumn of 1839, Walter Whitman (not yet Walt) was employed on a newspaper at Jamaica, Long Island. Recently he had edited his own paper at Huntington, but he was now working as printer and contributor on the *Long Island Democrat*. No file for this newspaper has survived, but any journalist near New York would have been aware of the great public excitement being created by the daguerreotype operators. By the spring of 1840 a man with the interesting name of Alexander Wolcott had opened a daguerreotype shop on Broadway at Chambers Street, and the following summer Morse and Draper built a small glass house on the top of the New York University building (it had only one) at Washington Square and began teaching the daguerreotype process, which they had improved, with typical American ingenuity, by lighting magnification to reduce the time of exposure. One of Morse's students was Mathew Brady.

In the summer of 1840 Whitman was teaching school at Woodbury, Long Island, and many years later a daguerreotype of him which he had given to a relative in Woodbury turned up. Because Whitman was teaching in Woodbury in 1840, Professor Emory Holloway assumed that it was made in that year, and so dated it when he reproduced it from a newspaper clipping in 1921 in his *Uncollected Poetry and Prose of Walt Whitman*. The 1840 date is a little improbable but not impossible. Before that year ended Brady had begun making daguerreotypes, and within a few months several "galleries" (the name emphasized the expected rivalry with painting) were opened not only in New York City but also in Boston, Philadelphia, Washington, Baltimore, and before long in every American city of any size. By the middle of the decade being daguerreotyped was the American rage, the thing to do, and the larger galleries developed assembly-line techniques so that everyone could afford to be "taken."

The Woodbury daguerreotype has been lost, but another, made about the same time, was kept by Whitman, and is now in the Walt Whitman House in Camden, N. J. [Plate 9]. In this early daguerreotype we see a supercilious young man with a neat beard—without moustache—wearing a fashionable coat and hat, a foulard tie, fondling a walking cane. He himself is obviously impressed by his natty appearance. This is the narcissistic young man who edited the New York *Aurora* for a few months in 1842, and it is not unlikely that this daguerreotype was taken during the time he was boasting in his editorials of parading up and down Broadway as a sophisticated observer of the *beau monde*. He mentions attending social affairs of all kinds, receptions, lectures, art exhibitions, prize fights, and sensational murder trials. A young apprentice on his paper recalled later that Whitman "usually wore a frock coat and high hat, carried a small cane, and the lapel of his coat was almost invariably ornamented with a boutonniere."

The other daguerreotype, possibly made while he was teaching school at Woodbury or nearby, exhibits the same fashionable clothes, but the face has a more callow expression. In a third daguerreotype we see a young man of about the same age, with similar dress, beard, and long hair, but he appears less assured—even unhealthy, though the facial expression may have been the result of the long exposure with his head pressed back against the required curved iron support. Of course the exposure was probably even longer for the other portraits, if they were earlier. Anyway, this is the pre-*Leaves of Grass* Whitman—Whitman before his metamorphosis.

The 1854 daguerreotype, which Dr. R. M. Bucke, Whitman's first biographer, called "the Christ likeness," shows the changing Whitman—chastened, introspective, benign [Plate 10]. But again this appearance may be partly the accidental, fleeting expression caught by the camera during a rigid pose. The daguerreotype which Whitman had engraved to be used as the frontispiece of his 1855 *Leaves of Grass* is probably of the same date and made by Mathew Brady's top camera man, Gabriel Harrison [Plate 11]. It is said to have been taken on a hot day in July, 1854—out of doors, we might guess, though the rigid standing pose would have been difficult to hold without support. The young man in shirt sleeves, collar open, hat tilted rakishly, strikes a nonchalant attitude, one hand on his hip and the other thrust into the pocket of his work-jeans. The Van Dyke beard is neatly trimmed, the handsome face half-smiles with a slightly amused expression, the eyes shrewdly alert. The pose is both defiant and ingratiating. This is the poet of the 1855 *Leaves of Grass* who signs his book with the engraving made from Harrison's daguerreotype. This would become the first Whitman icon.

In his 1856 edition Whitman reprinted his 1855 frontispiece, but in his third edition (1860) he used a steel engraving made from a portrait in oil painted by his friend Charles Hine. Photographs taken around 1860 indicate that Hine's portrait was probably painted in 1858 or 1859. The full face, the short beard, the luxuriant moustache are doubtless authentic, but the Byronic costume and wavy hair are artificial embellishments. This is the too-conscious poet, a would-be Victor Hugo.

A notebook which Whitman carried between 1858 and 1859, the period when he frequented Pfaff's Bohemian restaurant on lower Broadway, contains several crayon sketches of Whitman, which Jean Catel published as self-portraits. Recently Mrs. Florence Freedman pointed out that this sketch closely resembles an anonymous caricature of Whitman published in *Vanity Fair* on March 17, 1860. It seems likely that the notebook sketch was made by the artist assigned by *Vanity Fair* to caricature Whitman, and he willingly cooperated to obtain publicity for the third edition of his poems, which a Boston publisher had recently agreed to publish. The artist was probably a friend of Whitman, quite likely, as Mrs. Freedman conjectures, a drinking companion at Pfaff's. The 1859–1860 notebook also contains other humorous sketches of a man resembling Whitman in various stages of inebriation, and I suspect a congenial and convivial relationship between the poet and the artist.

By 1860 a new process of taking pictures on treated paper negatives, from which positive prints could be made, had nearly supplanted the cumbersome daguerreotype process, which gave only one picture for each exposure. Duplication could be achieved only by making an engraving from the daguerreotype or a lithographic copy, the latter cheaper than an engraving but less clear.

The new process was called "photography" to distinguish it from daguerreotypography. Brady had switched to photography, and his gallery on Broadway, near Barnum's "Museum," was now a showplace. To have one's photograph displayed on Brady's walls was a coveted distinction. In fact, several photographers had begun collecting photographs of famous people as contributions to social history. Whitman and Brady were good friends and often discussed the importance of photography. And either because he was well known as a former newspaper editor and author of a notorious book, or merely because he was photogenic, Whitman was often photographed in Brady's gallery. (Brady himself seldom operated a camera.) Other photographers also liked to "take" the picturesque poet, and from 1860 on the photographs of Whitman are abundant.

By the time Whitman reached Washington in 1862, Brady was proprietor of a large gallery in the Capitol, which continued operating while Brady himself was following the troops, trying to photograph their life in camp and on the battlefield during actual fighting. Some of the best Civil War photographs of Whitman were taken by Brady's firm in Washington while Brady was at the battlefront. They seem especially to record the lusty, robust Whitman, shaggy, confident and at ease, though overweight and a little too florid—even in a black-and-white print we can easily imagine the glowing cheeks which Whitman described in his letters to his mother [Plate 12]. Biographers agree that Whitman found the greatest happiness of his life in serving the wounded and convalescent soldiers in the hospitals, and the Brady photographs testify to this fact.

Whitman's favorite photo of this period, however, was taken in 1863 by Alexander Gardner, a Scotchman who operated a gallery in Washington [Plate 13]. Gardner was especially skillful in using light and shadow to bring out character. To me, the man in the Gardner portraits of 1863 is more intellectual, less sensual, more capable of writing *Drum-Taps* than the Brady images. But the photo of the man in the striped shirt (Whitman said a newspaper reporter called it his night shirt) who looks like Tolstoy is a Brady. In 1955 the Russians used a huge blowup of this photograph as a backdrop for a Whitman program in Moscow [Plate 14].

About 1869 Frank Pearsall of Brooklyn made a photograph of Whitman which later became one of the most widely published photos of the poet, sometimes called the "Moses picture" [Plate 15]. Here the pose, the black coat, the hypnotic eyes, and of course the face framed by the gray hair and beard, chin resting on hand, all contribute to the unworldly suggestion—one has to say "mystical." Two other photographs made about the same time and probably also by Pearsall have much the same effect, except that they remind one of a Hindu mystic instead of an Old Testament prophet. Even the more realistic photo by Pearsall in 1872, with the poet resting his elbow on a desk or table, has some of the same brooding quality, though with a difference [Plate 16]. In this photo the broad-brimmed, low-crowned hat and untied tie dangling below the unbuttoned collar give Whitman the fashion-defying appearance he had cultivated since 1855. It also conveys the impression of crude strength extolled in *Leaves of Grass*.

A photograph taken by G. C. Potter in Washington in 1871 so deeply impressed Whitman that he wrote a poem to illustrate it—a reversal of the usual order. [Plate 17.] The poem began:

> Out from behind this bending, rough-cut Mask
> (All straighter, liker Masks rejected—this preferr'd,)
> This common curtain of the face, . . .

The phrase "liker [that is, more like] Masks rejected" plainly indicates that the poet did not prefer this photo for being true-to-life. W. J. Linton made a woodcut from the photo which Whitman printed opposite the poem in his 1876 edition of *Leaves of Grass*. Professor Harold Blodgett has pointed out that in the earlier version of this poem Whitman had written (lines 13–15):

> From these to emanate, to you, who'er you are,
> These burin'd eyes—a Look.

Blodgett comments:

> "Burin'd" is of course a technical term meaning "cut by the burin," an engraver's tool for cutting, and Whitman must have at first greatly fancied the eyes of the Linton engraving, which are indeed brilliant and compelling. The odd fact is that, talking with Traubel in the late Eighties, Whitman repudiated these remarkable eyes as untrue to the reality. "My eyes are by no means bright, liquid, startling—no, not a bit of that sort of eyes: they are rather dull—rather sluggish—to be pictured, as I often say, by what they are not rather than by what they are." [*With Walt Whitman in Camden*, II, 144.] He was right, of course, as the testimony of others bears out [Edward Carpenter, *Days with Walt Whitman*, p. 6], but, after all, it is a mask of which the poet wrote in his poem—"all straighter, liker Masks rejected"— a symbol which embraces both Walt Whitman the actual and Walt Whitman the mythic, who are inseparable.

In 1879, while visiting New York to give his memorial Lincoln lecture, Whitman was photographed by Sarony, at that time the most fashionable photographer in New York, with a luxurious studio on Fifth Avenue. Here we see how much a photographer's expertise can contribute to the interpretation of character. The Sarony photos show the same kindly, bearded old man, but the lighting and texture of the print somehow give him an appearance of well-dressed prosperity. It is likely that Whitman had bought a new suit and hat for the trip, but someone had brushed his beard and made him feel contented with the world. Perhaps, too, Whitman enjoyed the brilliance of his surroundings, for his tastes were not always as simple as he liked to think.

Only one year later, Edy Brothers in London, Ontario, photographed Whitman with quite different results—and the difference is in the facial expression as well as in the shabby great coat he is wearing. Then a year later still (1881) while in Boston on another lecture trip, Whitman was photographed by Bartlett F. Kenny with an even more startling contrast to the Edy photograph. Whitman himself called this his "pompous photo," and for him it certainly was pompous. Of course he was more formally dressed than in Canada the previous year, but the starched shirt evidently affected his posture and facial expression—no doubt under encouragement from the camera man.

While Whitman was vacationing in Ocean Grove, N. J., in 1883, a Philadelphia photographic firm, Phillips and Taylor, took a photo of him which became almost a legend. The photograph shows him seated on a rustic bench holding his right hand aloft with a butterfly balanced on his forefinger [Plate 18]. The butterfly looks real, and was thought to be by many who saw the photograph, which Whitman used as a frontispiece in an 1889 edition of his *Leaves of Grass*. To the romantic-minded, here was a poet so close to nature that he could draw a butterfly to him and induce it to light on his finger. One of Esther Shephard's disillusionments was her discovery of a cardboard butterfly among Whitman's notebooks in the Library of Congress. It was wired to fit on the finger and was evidently the butterfly in the famous picture. Whitman had used a butterfly to decorate the back strips of the 1860 and 1881 editions.

Probably the most famous of all Whitman photographs, however, except for the 1855 frontispiece, was made by George C. Cox, one of the really great American photographers of the nineteenth century, though neglected by historians until recently. On the morning of April 15, 1887, Whitman's friends took him to Cox's studio at Broadway and 12th Street, where twenty or more pictures were taken of him. His favorite of all these was the one he called "the laughing philosopher," though the laughter was more internal than external [Plate 19]. Later T. Johnson made an etching of this photograph which was widely sold, printed, and imitated—note the seal on the *Walt Whitman Review*.

Ida Tarbell wrote of Cox in *McClure's Magazine* (IX, 560): "The subject who comes to him prepared to pose is surprised to be greeted with what seems to be quite irrelevant, though decidedly brilliant talk . . . ," Cox's theory being "that all men purposely or unwittingly wear a mask, and that unless this mask can be torn away and the emotions allowed to chase across the face, no characteristic picture is possible."

The success of Cox in getting Whitman to feel at ease on this occasion is described by W. S. Kennedy, who was present on this occasion, in his *Reminiscences of Walt Whitman:*

> He must have had twenty pictures taken, yet he never posed for a moment. He simply sat in the big revolving chair and swung himself to the right or to the left, as Mr. Cox directed, or he took his hat off or put it on again, his expression and attitude remaining so natural that no one would have supposed he was sitting for a photograph (p. 22).

Whitman may not have known it at the time, but one purpose of this visit was to enable Cox to take pictures of him which could be sold to help relieve his financial distress. This plan may also have helped to get this photograph so widely distributed, as well as the excellent etching made by Johnson.

Another photograph taken by Cox on that April morning in 1887 shows the grandfatherly old man with two children, the small nephew and niece of Jeannette L. Gilder, who had accompanied Whitman to the studio and brought the children [Plate 20]. This photograph was recently reproduced in the sumptous *American Album* (1968), edited by Jensen, Kerr, and Belsky, who make this comment:

> Of all the portraits of the great, near great, and famous made by George Collins Cox, only two were ever copyrighted. Both were of his friend Walt Whitman, and they were sold to raise money for the aging man of letters whose blazing pioneer poetry had been so rudely rejected by Victorian America. Whitman was deeply grateful. Other photographers, he once complained, "have used me as a show-horse again and again and again; they make pictures of me and sell them; but as for paying me—well they don't worry about that: all except Cox, the premier exception, who, I shouldn't wonder, has paid me as much as a hundred dollars and more in royalties." Cox paid him more than money; he paid Whitman, in this copyrighted character

analysis, the ultimate compliment of understanding the ageless unity of the "body electric." The year was 1887, Whitman, then sixty-seven, had just suffered a severe stroke; the children, Nigel and Catherine Jeannette Cholmeley-Jones, whom Cox visualized as soul-extensions of the first poet of the American spirit, would shortly be orphaned (to be raised by their aunt, Jeannette Leonard Gilder, the editor of the influential Critic.) Whitman was but five years from the "bitter hub of mortality."

Recent biographers believe that Whitman's story of having had six illegitimate children was a figment of his senile imagination, but he did love children, as this photograph shows. He reminds me of a mother cat purring to her kittens. A great "motherman," John Burroughs called him. In this photograph—and there are at least two others with different children very much like it—we have one of the most authentic images of Whitman.

Several Philadelphia photographers photographed Whitman during his residence in Camden. The most famous of these was Gutekunst, comparable in reputation and social prestige to Sarony in New York. One of Gutekunst's best of Whitman was made in 1889 [Plate 21]. It shows the poet looking tired and worn, considerably aged since the Cox photo that was made two years previously, but the patient eyes, the open collar making room for the flowing snow-white beard, the high-crowned, broad-brimmed hat—these characteristic details are all here, the real and the histrionic Whitman gracefully combined.

Thomas Eakins also photographed Whitman, both while he was painting him in 1887 and afterwards. One of his most successful attempts, a lighted profile against a dark background, was made in 1891 [Plate 22]. The head is venerable with age, but it is so without passion, so calm and resigned, that we might imagine it has attained a stasis in time.

II.

In 1877 George W. Waters painted the first of three portraits of Whitman in the home of the New York jeweler, J. H. Johnston, who then lived on East 10th Street. Waters had won national recognition the previous year for his landscapes shown at the Philadelphia Centennial Exhibition, especially for one of Franconia Notch, in the White Mountains. He was also well known for his portraits, and was much in demand for commissions to paint governors, judges, and famous people, including Joseph Jefferson, who had won fame and fortune in the role of Rip Van Winkle. Mr. Johnston had employed a fashionable artist to paint his friend Walt Whitman. The best known of these three portraits is perhaps a little idealized, but it gives a fairly convincing image of the poet after his partial recovery from his first stroke.

This same jeweler-friend was also responsible for bringing Whitman to New York a decade later to give his now-famous "Lincoln address" and to pose for photographers and another artist. Among Whitman's many friends who were invited was John Burroughs, who came down the Hudson to New York to hear the Lincoln lecture on April 14, 1887. Next day Burroughs recorded in his diary that at ten A.M. Walt "went to the photographers, with Jennie Gilder [and apparently others], and then to the studio of Miss Dora Wheeler for a sitting. Think Miss Wheeler will make a strong picture of him." Perhaps for the one sitting—Walt returned to Camden the next day (April 16), and I find no record of other sittings —her portrait was more than creditable, though rather bland and saccharine. Earlier that spring a much more famous painter, J. W. Alexander, had made sketches from which he later painted a full portrait of Whitman seated in a chair, in a saintly pose—as unrealistic as Miss Wheeler's and as refined as the Whitman in a Sarony photograph. Alexander's portrait was later given to the Metropolitan Museum in New York City [Plate 23].

During the following summer Sidney Morse, a roving sculptor who had failed to gain a foothold anywhere, moulded a bust of Whitman in modeling clay. His first attempt was not satisfactory to anyone, including himself, but a second highly pleased Whitman. Both, however, were cast in bronze, though no one bought either. Burroughs' impression was: "Morse made a big, shaggy sort of Homeric bust of him that had power, but he overdid it. He didn't show the womanliness there was in Walt— there was something fine, delicate, womanly in him" [Plate 24]. Burroughs probably meant the second bust, though his comment could have applied to either one. Whether we agree with Burroughs or not, the second bust was a little too obviously symbolic in its massive shagginess—and the first even more so. But Whitman always defended the second bust, perhaps because he liked Morse and sympathized with his hardships. Morse also modeled a life-size statue of Whitman seated in his favorite rocking chair, but it was never cast.

While Morse was busy in Walt's living room in Camden with his modeling clay, the son of the distinguished English woman who had tried to marry Whitman arrived from England to paint him. For some reason Whitman had never really liked Herbert Gilchrist, and he agreed to sit for a portrait mainly out of respect for the artist's mother. For several days both sculptor and painter tried to work in the small room, but finally Morse moved his operation out to the backyard, from which he made frequent trips back to the living room for another look at the poet sitting for the painter.

At the end of summer Gilchrist took his portrait back to London, exhibited it in the National Gallery, and was rewarded by being elected to the Royal Academy [Plate 25]. The *Pall Mall Gazette* printed a picture of his painting as one of the most distinguished portraits of the year. But Whitman refused to be impressed. He thought the portrait too refined, too "arty," perhaps, in part at least, because this was his opinion of the painter. He preferred Morse's second bust, and another portrait in oil painted by Thomas Eakins later in the year [Plate 26]. This was Walt Whitman's year in art: oil portraits by Wheeler and Gilchrist; sculptures, bas reliefs, and medallions by Morse; and sketches by Alexander for a full-length portrait completed two years later.

Today, of course, of these artists only Eakins has a great reputation— though even his depends upon the critic you read. In 1887 Eakins was generally disliked in art circles, even in his native Philadelphia. The Academy had dropped him from a teaching position not long before he met Whitman. He was thought to be crude, indecent, both as man and artist. He painted a society woman in the nude and then publicly exhibited the portrait. That was unforgivable! He was fascinated by the subtle play of athletes' muscles in action, especially of boxers. People said he was Rabelaisian, and his friendship with the author of *Leaves of Grass*, which had been banned in Boston, did not help his reputation in "respectable" Philadelphia. But Walt was not shocked by Rabelais and he adored Tom Eakins.

Herbert Gilchrist sailed for England several months before Eakins began painting Whitman, and he could only imagine what the finished portrait looked like. In a conversation with Traubel on May 14, 1888, Walt reported:

> "Herbert says he is sure he would not like Eakins' picture: all Eakins' methods, he says, are tortuous. What do you take Herbert to mean by that? Tortuous? How?" W. argued oppositely: "The Eakins por-

trait gets there—fulfils its purpose; sets me down in correct style, without feathers—without any fuss of any sort. I like the picture always—it never fades—never weakens. Now, Herbert is determined to make me the conventional, proper old man: his picture is never benevolent, to be sure; but the Walt Whitman of that picture lacks guts." Harned said: "He gave you curls in your beard." "Yes, and more too: much more. You can see what Herbert made of me by the remarks of some of the visitors—two women—who were surprised to find that Walt Whitman was not after all a wild man but a rather tame man—almost a man of the world. But you see how it is. The world insists on having its own way: it don't want a man so much the way he looks as the way it is accustomed to having men look." After conversation in this vein we discussed the question of the ownership of the Eakins picture (half of it Walt's, E. had said), Walt remarking with a laugh: "But I'll kick the bucket some day—no doubt very soon now—and then some of these things will be of some value and be sought after."

Whatever the merits of his opinions on art, Whitman was right about the value of these paintings after his death. Without attempting to evaluate these as art, we can observe some of the differences in the interpretations of the poet's character and personality by these three artists. Alexander presents a charming old man, almost angelic in his white whiskers, immaculate cuffs, saintly face, contrasting starkly with the priestly black gown and dark background. In Eakins' portrait we see a rosy-cheeked, jolly Dutchman—not so much Rabelaisian as the "caresser of life," to use one of Whitman's phrases. Some of the Brady photographs of the early 1860s give us glimpses of this Whitman, but Eakins heightened the Dutch inheritance from the poet's mother, which he himself took more pride in than his English inheritance from his father. Because Eakins did not know Whitman in his prime, it is a little remarkable that he could see this innate character (perhaps strongest in the decade of the 1860s) in the old man he painted in 1887.

Of these three artists, Gilchrist actually painted a more realistic portrait than either Eakins or Alexander—a face with benevolence (Whitman to the contrary) but ravaged by age and physical suffering. This face is also flushed, but less from *joie de vivre* than high blood pressure. As for the fashionable *style*, if it has such, this might be the tricks with light— the golden reflections and glittering spots of reddish light in the whole composition. The collar edged with lace in the Eakins portrait (scarcely recognizable in Gilchrist's) actually seems more effeminate than the slightly curly beard painted by Gilchrist, though of these two details, the lacy collar was more literally true to life, for Whitman did pose in a shirt on which his doting housekeeper had sewed the lace seen in the portrait. They are all *icons:* Alexander's saint, Eakins' Dutchman, Gilchrist's glowing grandfather with an air of sly reserve. And so, too, is Morse's Homeric head in the crude, massive bust.

But the final *icon* might be said to be a photograph taken by Eakins in 1891. This venerable head in profile with dark background was used for an etching by Jacques Reich, which Whitman's literary executors published as the frontispiece of Volume I of the 1902 edition of Whitman's so-called *Complete Writings.* Here we see the old poet a few months before his death, calm and resigned in spite of his physical suffering. He is the aged phoenix ready for the fire of regeneration—fearless and ready. If he is Lao-tzu reincarnated, as H. S. Saunders suggests in his Whitman album, what, one wonders, will be his next incarnation?

III.

During Whitman's Centennial in 1919 newspapers and magazines published many articles on him and his *Leaves of Grass,* a considerable number illustrated by photographs and both pen and crayon drawings. Throughout the twenties this interest was kept alive mainly by two men, Cleveland Rodgers, editor of the Brooklyn *Daily Eagle,* which Whitman had once edited, and Professor Emory Holloway. Through the *Eagle* Rodgers conducted an intermittent campaign to get Whitman admitted to the New York University Hall of Fame. In 1925, after Whitman had several times failed to get enough votes, a bust was smuggled in one night and set up both as a joke and a publicity stunt. The following year Whitman's reputation was enhanced by the publication of Holloway's biography, which won a Pulitzer Prize.

In 1926 a new hotel in Camden, N. J., was named for the town's famous resident during his last years, and Whitman's physician, Dr. Alexander McAlister, headed a committee to employ a distinguished artist to memorialize him in a mural. The Artists Alliance of Philadephia conducted a competition, which was won by the Philadelphia artist, Robert E. Johnston, and he was given the commission to paint a large mural for the main lobby of the hotel. As might be expected, the mural he produced was highly symbolical, presenting Whitman as a semidivine figure silently "charging" the men and women of various occupations with his spiritual power—as he dreamed of doing in his 1855 Preface and "Song of Myself." Another Philadelphia artist, W. G. Krieghoff, who had also submitted designs in the contest, was commissioned to paint five lunette panels over the doorways of the ballroom. In style and subject matter they resembled the mural. The Walt Whitman Hotel closed in February, 1969, and probably these paintings will be destroyed.

In 1930 Whitman was finally elected to the Hall of Fame—just barely! Mr. Rodgers and others raised funds to commission a bust. The sculptor employed was Chester Beach, and his bust was unveiled and dedicated on May 14, 1930, along with busts of the geographer Matthew Maury, President Monroe, and James McNeill Whistler. Beach probably modeled the head from photographs of Whitman taken in the period between 1869 and 1872. I see a close resemblance to one of the unmystical Pearsall photos of 1869. The stiff dignity of the poet in the bust, and a somewhat stern expression, fits his honorable position in the Hall of Fame overlooking the Harlem River.

It was also about 1930 that Alexander Finta, a sculptor whose works may be seen in various public places in New York City, did a bronze plaque to mark the building where the first *Leaves of Grass* was printed in Brooklyn, at the corner of Fulton and Cranberry Streets. (That building was torn down several years ago and the plaque is now in the Whitman Birthplace at Huntington.) Later Mr. Finta completed several heads and busts in plaster which were included in an exhibition of his work at the Library of Congress in 1939.

During the 1930s, most artists were unemployed, and many of those given temporary employment by the New York City W. P. A. Project selected Walt Whitman as a subject. Perhaps the most outstanding of these was Ben Shahn, who used Whitman in his large murals for a new Bronx Post Office building. One of these showed Whitman seated at a desk, surrounded by ten men and youths, pointing to a blackboard which displayed some lines from "As a Strong Bird on Pinions Free." A professor of ethics at Fordham University strongly objected to the poet's teaching his audience

> To formulate the Modern— . . .
> Out of thyself, comprising science, to recast poems,
>   churches, art,
> (Recast, may-be discard them, end them—may-be their
>   work is done, who knows?)

A storm of controversy resulted from the priest's objection, but Shahn calmed it by offering to erase the blackboard and substitute a less provocative quotation.

This incident gives a clue to the attitude of people in the 1930s to Whitman in art: both to the artists and the public he was either "the poet of democracy," something like Edwin Markham, or the poet of the proletarian revolution, or both combined. Rough features, heroic size, and bulging muscles, the trademark shaggy hair and beard, an enraptured expression on his face—these were the visual details emphasized in busts, statues, medallions, paintings, and everything else. Some of these were indeed excellent interpretations of a simplified Whitman, such as Warren Wheelock's small plaster statuette of the poet with upraised arms joyously greeting (or blessing?) the Promised Land. It gives such illusion of size that a photograph makes it look like a larger-than-life statue.

The idea behind the famous ten-foot bronze Whitman made by Jo Davidson, now in the Bear Mountain State Park, originated in a plan Professor Holloway had for erecting a statue of Whitman at Battery Park on the tip of Manhattan Island [Plate 27]. This plan was eventually abandoned, but not before Davidson had become interested and made a preliminary model in his Paris studio, where it finally attracted the attention of Mr. Averell Harriman, then president of the Union Pacific Railroad. He commissioned the statue to be completed and erected as a memorial to his mother at the beginning of the Appalachian Trail at Bear Mountain. But the statue was first exhibited at the New York World Fair in 1939, then moved to its permant site the following year. Mr. Davidson used Morse's bust as a model for the head, though the features in Davidson's head are less rough than Morse's and more closely resemble the Whitman of Cox's photographs. Whitman's "Song of the Open Road" suggested the walking posture, which is especially appropriate for the permanent site—a granite hilltop beside a woodland trail.

There are many other busts, statues, and statuettes of Whitman, both older and more recent ones. One of the more unusual pieces is a colossal head five feet tall created by the late Simon Gordon of welded small steel rectangles. As the editor of the *Walt Whitman Review* says, "Simon Gordon felt that Walt Whitman represented all men, and therefore the head should be larger than life."

Another large statue, but full-length, stands at the entrance to the Ingersoll Building which houses the Brooklyn Public Library. It is a bronze by Thomas Hudson Jones, erected in 1939. The face might be said to be of Whitman around 1860, but the conventional clothes, close-trimmed beard, and aggressive face look more like a prosperous merchant or owner of a newspaper than the Brooklyn editor-poet before the Civil War. One feels that the sculptor has tried to make his fellow-townsman respectable.

During the winter of 1968 and 1969 the Brooklyn Museum exhibited a little-known head of Whitman carved out of tan-colored Barrie granite by Ahron Ben-Shmuel during the Public Works assistance to artists in the 1930s. It shows a strong influence of William Blake, and gives an impressive image of Whitman as mystic or prophet.

IV.

Earlier I mentioned the first known caricatures of Whitman published in *Vanity Fair* in 1860. The next surviving datable caricature appeared in *The Fifth Avenue Journal* in 1872 in a series called "Men of the Day." Inclusion in this series was a distinct honor to Whitman, the result, evidently, of his having opened the National Industrial Exhibition the previous autumn with a poem, "After All, Not to Create Only," which most of the New York newspapers printed next day. It was also widely commented upon in the press, though for the most part satirically.

In the spring of 1872 Whitman delivered a poem at Dartmouth College, "As a Strong Bird on Pinions Free," which was also extensively publicized. Though not yet widely accepted in his own country as an important poet, in 1872 Walt Whitman was recognized in New York City as a man of prominence—perhaps even a celebrity. This caricature is not cruel. The caricaturist, Frank Bellew, only slightly increases the abundance of hair and beard and the size of the head (the main comic feature). The floppy hat, open collar, and slack necktie are in the early 1870 photographs of Whitman.

A scrapbook of John McLennon in the New York Public Library contains a much more exaggerated crayon sketch of Whitman's big hat, wild hair and beard, and open collar, with the inscription: "This head Ladies and Gentlemen shows the want of knowledge. Parents selecting a profession suitable for youth—Here is a case in point: Gifted by nature, this subject with a head that is swollen with literary talent—Is allowed to go to grass—With all the fire and fancy of a Byron &c. This subject has been toiling, dealing and pining over and amongst Clams, Shedders and Yaups from childhood up—Sir turn your attention to Literature—and the Temple of Fame will have an occupant, shure."

An artist named Fornaro (possibly a pseudonym) satirized the "Butterfly Photo" with a sketch of a clown with Whitman's beard and hat, balancing a butterfly on a forefinger held aloft like a flagpole. Whitman had used the "Butterfly Photo" as the frontispiece for his 1889 *Leaves of Grass*. Another caricature was used by the half-Japanese, half-German young man named Sadakichi Hartmann who visited Whitman during his last years. The cover of Hartmann's thin volume of *Conversations with Walt Whitman* (1895) displayed an ink drawing of the over-eager Sadakichi and a bored Walt Whitman. But the masterpiece of all Whitman caricatures was made in 1904 by Max Beerbohm, representing the paunchy, earth-bound Whitman manfully "inciting the bird of freedom to soar." The scrawny eagle, about the size of a crow, does not get the idea [Plate 28].

In 1921 Van Verveke drew a picture for *The New York Times Book Review* (June 26, 1921, p. 13) of "Mrs. Browning, Tennyson, Walt Whitman, and Ossian in consultation over a group of ultra modern poets." Two years later (June 10, 1923, p. 3) Oscar Cesare drew a Rip-van-Winkle-looking Whitman tramping past an indifferent, sybaritic man with the face of a Sinclair Lewis to illustrate this sentence: "The young intellectuals seem to be looking back; their vision of the future is lost in a painfully general assumption that things have crystalized as they are."

In 1925 Fred Lewis in the *New York Herald Tribune Magazine* (September 13, 1925, p. 8) represented Poe and Whitman commiserating over the posthumous price of their books:

> Quoth Walt Whitman: "I see by the papers that first editions of my 'Leaves of Grass' fetch $250.00 these days."
>
> Quoth the Raven: "Croak! a 25 cent copy of our 'Tamerlain' just sold for $12,500!"

Some of the ultra-modern paintings of Whitman appear to me to be caricatures, too, but this may be my limited point of view. For example, Carl Holty's colorful "abstract" in a sort of "futuristic-cubistic" style: the big hat and the cane are familiar, but the misshapen face (unrecognizable without the label) and the pot-bellied man straining the chair he sits on look to me like a Marxist cartoon of the capitalistic plutocrat.

V.

When we come to what I will call "Whitman in Commercial Art," we find much greater misrepresentation than in even the most unkind caricatures of him. I call it "commercial" because the artist does not really know Whitman, has studied photographs hastily and superficially, and uses Whitman as a subject only to cash in on his name and reputation. The result is that Whitman is distorted in some very uncharacteristic way —unlike the caricature which exaggerates a characteristic physical appearance, habit, or eccentricity. Often in the commercial artist's representation of Whitman we would not recognize the man unless we were given his name. During World War II the United States Government published a comic strip magazine with a six-page sequence on "Walt Whitman: Bard of Democracy." In none of the frames is there a good representation of Whitman's face. As a little boy he has yellow hair, as a young man he is a clean-shaven All-American boy, and as a nurse in the Civil War hospitals he resembles James Russell Lowell. As a matter of fact, he is dressed like Lowell too.

In the John Hancock advertisement using Whitman, the face has some resemblance to the poet in old age, with snow-white hair, and he does carry in his hand the battered Whitman hat, but the prosperous, well-preserved, theatrical man striding over the hill is a burlesque of Jo Davidson's poet of the "Open Road." The commercialized Whitman is almost invariably sentimentalized, conventionalized, slicked up, idealized— but materially, not spiritually as in the Alexander portrait, which is not commercial art.

Most illustrators of fancy editions of Whitman's poems, such as Rockwell Kent and Boardman Robinson, commit the same offenses. For the color plates for the Illustrated Modern Library edition of *Leaves of Grass* (1944), Robinson must have used Uncle Remus as his model rather than a photograph or portrait from life. The high coloring suggests Eakins' Jolly Dutchman, but if one places Boardman Robinson's illustrations beside Eakins' portrait, he will see the difference between esthetic art (to use a redundancy) and commercial art. However, as the nadir in commercial art—if there is a nadir—I think of the cover of a paperback edition to which I contributed an Introduction: the Signet *Leaves of Grass*. Here, unfortunately, the artist did catch some of Whitman's sly perversity. The face reminds me of Allen Ginsberg's Whitman, a "childless, lonely old grubber, poking among the meats in the refrigerator [in the California supermarket] and eyeing the grocery boys." I don't know whether this was intended or not by the Signet illustrator, but he drew the most repulsive Whitman I have ever seen in any graphic or plastic representation of him, and there are many other unattractive ones.

James Daugherty's illustrations for his very fine juvenile *Walt Whitman's America* serve their purpose well, for Daugherty had read Whitman with sympathy and understanding. His drawings do come near being caricatures in their magnification of the poet's heroic appearance and muscular body, which was in reality large but not muscular. Yet Daugherty merely dramatizes Whitman's own dream of his role as poet and national spokesman.

There are a few interesting illustrations for specific poems. In 1901 Jacob Epstein made a series of drawings to illustrate the "Calamus" poems [Plate 29]. The fact that so great an artist would even be interested in this attempt seems to me significant. I have seen reproductions of only three of these drawings, and the originals may be far superior. At first glance these three seem only studies of nude male torsos, but on looking closer we see lonely figures reaching out for contact with other lonely figures—which is perhaps the most basic emotion of these poems. I remember that "A Noiseless Patient Spider" was originally a "Calamus" poem, the spider, like the poet, reaching for anchorage in the immensity of space. An edition of the "Calamus" poems with Epstein's drawings might be an artistic and critical (interpretative) treasure.

In 1919 the French biographer and translator of Whitman, Léon Bazalgette, published a small selection of Whitman's poems with some rather exotic woodcuts by Franz Massereel on the "Calamus" theme [Plate 30]. The poet in these woodcuts is the 1854–1855 "Christ likeness," not the "Victor Hugo" of the 1860 edition, in which the "Calamus" group first appeared. The anachronism, however, is not important. The earlier image is more convincing for the poet who confesses that he is puzzled at himself, "conscience-struck," "self-convicted," secretly loving strangers, "O tenderly, a long time, and never avow it. . . ." Massereel's tropical vegetation and innocent lamb remind one of the symbolical scenery and fanciful creatures in Henri Rousseau's colorful canvases, and the exotic setting is more appropriate than a realistic swamp on Long Island, where Whitman saw the Calamus plant growing. Massereel's woodcuts are the most imaginative graphic interpretations of these poems I know. David Hockney's anonymous disembodied heads (unhoused by abstraction, to paraphrase Ransom's poem) and upside-down tree to illustrate "I Saw in Louisiana a Live-Oak Growing" is a little too apocalyptic.

A painting which I find difficult to classify is a mural by Gil Wilson for the Community Theatre in Terre Haute, Indiana. I mention it here because the artist was illustrating the *Drum-Taps* poem "Vigil Strange I Kept on the Field One Night"—vigil for a soldier who had died in battle. In Wilson's bright mural, with conscious borrowings from Blake, the poet holds his wake beside—almost over—the open grave of the fallen comrade. The dawn is breaking at the poet's back but some mysterious light illuminates his ancient (Blakesque) face.

VI.

I remarked earlier that some of the modern paintings of Whitman impressed me as caricatures, though presumably they were intended to be serious portraits. Another puzzling example is a canvas by Merton Clivette, a celebrity magician, author, and caricaturist of the early twentieth century. I have seen only a small photograph of the painting in the catalog of the sale of George S. Hellman's Collection in 1932. The catalog description reads:

> Clivette claimed to have known Whitman. A smaller portrait by Clivette of the poet is in the Carl W. Hamilton collection. The present canvas, broadly and rapidly painted, shows Clivette's fantastic capacity of giving, by the simplest means, expression to the human eye. It is probably the most fascinating of all paintings of Walt Whitman.

The eyes *are* expressive (like those in the Linton woodcut), and so is the nose, which is the feature that seems caricatured to me, giving the whole face a predatory look. I suppose the painter's style would be called impressionistic—possibly a clue to the date.

About twenty years ago the German artist Otto Pankok made a woodcut of Whitman which I venture to call expressionist. I also find it slightly amusing, and yet not unsympathetic. The face *is* Whitman's, and it has great expression (in the nontechnical sense), but what it expresses I would not try to say.

In the 1940s an Argentine edition of Armando Vasseur's translation of some of Whitman's poems into Spanish (originally published in Spain in 1912) was illustrated by the artist who signed himself "Carybé." I finally learned from the Hispanic Foundation of the Library of Congress that Carybé is the pseudonym of Hector Julio Paride Bernabo, now living in Bahia, Brazil, where he is a very famous painter and author. Carybé made about a dozen remarkable line drawings for the Vasseur translation [Plate 31]. He seems to have two conceptions of Whitman: (1) a giant among pygmies and (2) a mystic—a John the Baptist type living in the desert, on locusts and wild honey, no doubt. Both interpretations I find very impressive, though the giant is more familiar to me, one of Brady's photographs having rather obviously served as model for the face. The mystic is so wild with his inspiration that he is almost terrifying. However, both interpretations show great insight into Whitman's contradictions.

Several years later (1947) a Norwegian artist, Kai Fjell, gave a different interpretation, no less startling and revealing, made for the cover and frontispiece of a brilliant Norwegian translation of "Song of Myself" [Plate 32]. Perhaps because he was illustrating this poem, Fjell based his interpretation of the poet's character and appearance on the 1854 daguerreotype—the "Christ likeness," similar to the frontispiece of the 1855 *Leaves*. Both Carybé and Fjell use symbolism, but Fjell's is perhaps more subtle—with a Norse mysteriousness. I am not sure I entirely understand it, but the sailor with the Christ-like face is bound to a ship, sinking, it appears. Below deck, like captive Africans in a slave ship, are tortured human beings, whom I suppose in some way the bound sailor is trying to save—or bless before their watery death. I am not sure which. But it is a haunting image of the messianic poet in "Song of Myself."

Leonard Baskin's 1955 woodcut is, perhaps, also symbolical, but in a very different way. Baskin's Whitman is of the 1860s, or, more accurately, a particular photograph which has been variously dated but was probably made in Boston in the spring of 1860 while Whitman was seeing his third edition through the press. This Whitman is lanky, with a face the artist deliberately unbalanced. The distortion gives the poet a meager, loose-in-the-knees, ascetic look. There was such a Whitman, and this is an authentic icon—one of the many true ones.

To come from Carybé, Fjell, and Baskin to Antonio Frasconi is like coming back from realms of fantasy to solid earth. In 1960 Frasconi published a remarkable little book filled with woodcuts which he called *A Whitman Portrait*. It is indeed a visual biography, supplemented by short prose and verse selections which either help to explain, or are explained by, the series of marvelous woodcut portraits. Most of the portraits are based with considerable care on well-known photographs, but they have not been mechanically imitated [See frontispiece].

Charles Welles also made some fine etchings of Whitman, one based on the 1854 daguerreotype ("Christ likeness") and the other without any particular photographic source but depicting a slightly older (say of the late 1850s or early 1860s), wiser, shrewder, and possibly a sadder man. Welles has done especially well with the sensuous mouth (partly or wholly concealed in many of the photographs), the firm nose, and the sad eyes. This is not the Whitman popularly and superficially known, but one I came to know in writing *The Solitary Singer*.

VII.

The major images—or *icons*—of Whitman which stand out in my study of the numerous photographs and a wide range of both graphic and plastic representations of him are the following four:

1. The "Christ likeness" of 1854, one of the two daguerreotypes made by Gabriel Harrison that year, the bust (which Bucke called "Christ likeness") and the full-length portrait used as a frontispiece from the 1855 *Leaves of Grass*. The two images might be called a composite icon.

2. The Brady Whitman of 1863 (and again there are several photographs which show the same full-faced, voluptuous-lipped, steady-eyed man who looks brimming with health and vitality). In one photograph he wears a broad-brimmed hat (F. O. Matthiessen reproduced it in his *American Renaissance*, and the Grove Press used it for the cover of my illustrated *Walt Whitman*). This is the Whitman who was in reality the "wound dresser."

3. For a third *icon*, I choose without hesitation the "Moses" photograph of 1869. Another photo taken by Pearsall in 1869 also gives the image of a mystic, but the "Moses" picture is more famous.

4. The "Laughing Philosopher" in the Cox photograph of 1887, of which T. Johnson made a widely circulated etching. This image has probably been reprinted (both from the Cox photograph and the Johnson etching), imitated, or adapted more than any other image of Walt Whitman.

Of these four *icons*, two have definite religious connotations ("Christ" and "Moses"), and the Cox image suggests a "prophet"—or, in some of the adaptations, St. Nicholas. Only the Brady photo gives a wholly secular image of a sensual man in the prime of life. This is my favorite of the poet who, as Professor Edwin Miller says in *Walt Whitman's Poetry*, "sensualized the soul." But the "Christ likeness" continues to gain favor because the critics are increasingly finding the "essential

150   THE ARTISTIC LEGACY OF WALT WHITMAN

Whitman" in his first edition. This icon also appeals because of its suggestion of pathos. The "Moses" and "Laughing Philosopher" icons are somewhat sentimental—and they look *posed*—but they will continue to be cherished by idolators who worship the man more than his poetry.

These remarks are, of course, personal and subjective, but I am sure that I am statistically right about the *four icons*, representing "the outsetting bard," " the wound dresser," the "Passage to India" mystic, and the serene Walt Whitman in old age, of whom the Canadian psychiatrist R. M. Bucke said, "he looked like a god."

Notes

Professor Emory Holloway has supplied me with many newspaper clippings from his files, especially useful information on Whitman's election to the Hall of Fame, the Jo Davidson statue, and the work of Alexander Finta. He also permitted me to use two unpublished manuscripts he had written on George W. Waters and his friend Mr. Finta. Mr. and Mrs. Fred Tuten visited "Carybé" (Hector Julio Paride Bernabo) in Brazil and brought back personal information for me. The Hispanic Foundation of the Library of Congress supplied printed information on Carybé. I am most grateful to Mr. Tony Keys for his excellent photograph of the Jo Davidson statue in winter, and to the Brooklyn Museum and Professor Arthur Golden for a photograph of Ahron Ben-Schmuel's bust of Whitman. Mr. Gil Wilson kindly sent me photographs of his paintings and a sculpture (unfinished). Mr. John Davenport loaned me his copy of Saunder's *Whitman Portraits*—510. My colleague Edwin Miller has aided in various ways and is responsible for my undertaking this study—preliminary in its present form.

Sources

I. History and Whitman photographs:

Robert Taft, *Photography and the American Scene* (New York, 1938). Beaumont Newhall, *The History of Photography from 1839 to the Present Day* (New York, 1964). Oliver Jensen, Joan Patterson Kerr, and Murray Belsky, *American Album* (New York, 1968).

Henry S. Saunders, *Whitman Portraits* (Toronto, 1922—private edition, 510 photographs). Information about Whitman photographs in *With Walt Whitman in Camden,* five volumes published in different places, dates, and publishers. Jean Downey, "Walt Whitman Iconography" (unpublished M.A. thesis, supervised by GWA). Newspaper clippings.

Frontispiece in 1855 *Leaves of Grass:* Clifton Joseph Furness, Introduction to Facsimile Text Society Edition of *Leaves of Grass: First Edition (1855)* (New York, 1939). Gay Wilson Allen, *The Solitary Singer: A Critical Biography of Walt Whitman* (New York, 1955), p. 150.

Jean Catel, *Walt Whitman: la Naissance du Poète* (Paris, 1929).

Florence B. Freedman, "Caricatures in Picture and Verse: Walt Whitman in Vanity Fair, 1860," *Walt Whitman Review,* X (1964), 18–19, 23.

Harold W. Blodgett, "Whitman and the Linton Portrait," *Walt Whitman Review,* IV (1958), 90–92.

Butterfly photo: Esther Shephard, *Walt Whitman's Pose* (New York, 1938), p. 228. See also, *Solitary Singer,* pp. 512–14.

Cox: Marchal E. Landgren, "George C. Cox: Whitman's Photographer," *Walt Whitman Review,* IX (1963), 11–15, [23–24]; Clara Barrus, *Whitman and Burroughs: Comrades* (Boston, 1931).

II. Paintings and sculptures:

Eakins: *Walt Whitman in Camden,* esp. Vol. II, *passim.* Lloyd Goodrich, *Thomas Eakins: His Life and Work* (New York, 1933).

Waters: J. H. Johnston's letter to Charles N. Eliot (ed.), *Walt Whitman as Man, Poet and Friend* (Boston, 1915). Emory Holloway, unpublished essay.

Gilchrist: Oil painting of Whitman in Rare Book Department of University of Pennsylvania Library. Whitman's opinion on Herbert Gilchrist, *With Walt Whitman in Camden,* Vol. V, *passim.*

Finta: *Brooklyn Eagle,* June 25, 1939, and other clippings. Emory Holloway, unpublished manuscript.

III. Busts and statues:

Davidson: Jo Davidson statue at World's Fair, *Brooklyn Eagle,* May 31, 1939. *The New York Times.* June 1, 1939, and other New York newspapers.

Murals in Walt Whitman Hotel, *Camden Courier,* June 1, 1926.

Hall of Fame: *Brooklyn Eagle, The New York Times,* and other papers, May 15, 1931.

IV. Caricatures:

Saunders (see I above); Downey (I above); Print Room of New York Public Library.

V. Illustrations:

Walt Whitman Bard of Democracy comic book advertising U.S. Bonds, no publisher, place, or date given.

John Hancock, painting by William Smith, for John Hancock Life Insurance advertisements in magazines in 1955.

Rockwell Kent, illustrations for Heritage Club edition of *Leaves of Grass* (New York, 1937).

Boardman Robinson, the Illustrated Modern Library edition of *Leaves of Grass* (New York, 1944).

Signet: New American Library edition of *Leaves of Grass* (New York, 1958).

James Daugherty, *Walt Whitman's America* (New York, 1967).

Epstein: letter to author from Lady Epstein. *The Works of Sir Jacob Epstein, from the Collection of Mr. Edward P. Schinman* (Fairleigh Dickinson University Press, 1967), pp. 18, 42.

Léon Bazalgette (ed.), *Calamus: Poèmes*, avec 10 bois hors-texte dessinés et gravés par Frans Massereel (Genève, 1919).

Hockney: *Art and Literature*, 5 (Summer, 1965).

Gil Wilson, correspondence with author, photographs, postal card illustration of Terre Haute mural.

Clivette: Sale of George S. Hellman collection, December 14, 1932, American Art Association: Anderson Galleries, Inc. (New York, 1932).

Carybé: *Walt Whitman, Poemas, Versión de Armando Vasseur*, con diez ilustraciones del pintor Carybé y dos fotografias fuera de texto (Buenos Aires, [1943]).

Fjell: *Walt Whitman: Sangen om Meg Selv*, oversettelse og innledning ved Per Arneberg, tegninger av Kai Fjell (Oslo, 1947).

Baskin: cover of *Harvard Advocate*, Vol. XCVII (Spring, 1963).

Frasconi: *A Whitman Portrait*, Woodcuts by Antonio Frasconi (New York, 1960).

A Backward Glance:
A Bibliography of
Gay Wilson Allen

The Early Years

My *first* publication was an essay on the opossum which won some sort of prize in *The Progressive Farmer*, when I was around fourteen or fifteen. I remember the prize, for it was a volume of Emerson's essays—I think the first major work in American literature I read thoroughly.

In college I wrote dozens of feature stories for the student newspaper, the two daily newspapers in Durham, North Carolina, and one summer for the *Asheville Times* (the Sunday issue). The latter ran to four or five columns every Sunday.

Then as editor of the Duke *Chronicle* I wrote two or three editorials—sometimes six—a week and a column called "The Crow's Nest." Some members of the community, both students and faculty, publicly expressed the hope that I would fall out of the "nest" and break my g. d. neck. But I didn't.

I became so notorious that I was offered, unsolicited, three newspaper jobs when I graduated. But notoriety is relative. I almost caused a riot by advocating in an editorial that coeds be permitted to smoke. In 1938 when I returned to Duke to teach in summer school, it was the accepted custom for girls to smoke in class. I suspect my other outrageous opinions were equally tame—at least from the perspective of the present aggrieved college generation. It was not until I found a congenial berth on the New York University faculty that I stopped wondering if I should not have taken one of those newspaper jobs.

—Gay Wilson Allen

The Later Years

I. Books

American Prosody. New York: American Book Company, 1935. 342 pp.
New York: Octagon Books, 1966.

Literary Criticism: Pope to Croce, edited with H. H. Clark. New York:
American Book Company, 1941. 659 pp. Detroit: Wayne State University Press, 1961.

Twenty-Five Years of Walt Whitman Bibliography: 1918–1942. Boston:
F. W. Faxon Company, 1943. 57 pp.

Walt Whitman Handbook. Chicago: Packard and Company. 1946. 560
pp. New York: Hendricks House, 1958, 1962.

Masters of American Literature, edited with Henry A. Pochmann, 2 vols.
New York: The Macmillan Company, 1949. Reprint of Introductions:
Introduction to Masters of American Literature. Carbondale and Edwardsville, Illinois: Southern Illinois University Press. London and Amsterdam: Feffer & Simons, Inc., 1969. 156 pp.

"Introduction to Frederik Schyberg and His Walt Whitman," in Frederik
Schyberg, *Walt Whitman,* translated by Evie Allison Allen. New York:
Columbia University Press, 1951.

The Solitary Singer: A Critical Biography of Walt Whitman. New York:
The Macmillan Company, 1955. 616 pp. New York: Grove Press,
1959. London: John Calder, Ltd., 1959. New York: New York University Press, 1968.

Walt Whitman Abroad: Critical Essays from Germany, France, Scandinavia, Russia, Italy, Spain and Latin America, Israel, Japan, and India
(edited in translations). Syracuse, New York: Syracuse University Press,
1955. 290 pp.

Walt Whitman's Poems: Selections with Critical Aids, edited with Charles
T. Davis. New York: New York University Press, 1955, 1969. 280 pp.

"Walt Whitman: Man, Poet, Philosopher," in *Three Lectures Presented
Under the Auspices of the Gertrude Clarke Whittall Poetry and Literature Fund.* Washington, D. C.: The Library of Congress, 1955. Pp.
1–14. Reprinted, 1969.

"Introduction to the Mentor Edition" of *Leaves of Grass.* New York:
New American Library, 1958. Pp. v–xx. Reprinted, Signet edition, 1960.

Walt Whitman: Evergreen Profile Book (with over 70 illustrations). New
York: Grove Press, 1961. 192 pp. London: John Calder, Ltd., 1961.
Walt Whitman: Revised Edition. Detroit: Wayne State University
Press, 1969. 252 pp. Translation: *Walt Whitman in Selbstzeugnissen
und Bilddokumenten.* Herausgegeben von Kurt Kusenberg. Hamburg:
Rowohlt Verlag, 1961. 177 pp.

Walt Whitman as Man, Poet, and Legend. With a Check List of Whitman
Publications 1945–1960, by Evie Allison Allen. Carbondale, Illinois:
Southern Illinois University Press, 1961. 260 pp.

American Poetry, edited with Walter B. Rideout and James K. Robinson. New York: Harper & Row, 1965. 1274 pp.

William James, a Biography. New York: Viking Press, 1967. 556 pp. London: Rupert Hart-Davis, 1967. New York: Compass Book (Viking), 1969.

A Reader's Guide to Walt Whitman. New York: Farrar, Straus and Company, 1970.

Herman Melville and His World (A Studio Book). New York: The Viking Press, 1970.

Chapters or Reprinted Selections in Books

Encyclopaedia Britannica, 1960 edition: 20 articles on prosodic and literary terms, including (more important) "Free Verse," "Metre," and "Walt Whitman"; 1962 edition: long article on "Figures of Speech" (a new entry in *E. B.*).

"Walt Whitman," in *The Reader's Encyclopedia of American Literature*. Edited by Max J. Herzberg. New York: Thomas Y. Crowell Company, 1962. Pp. 1222–26.

"Henry James, Sr." and "William James," in *The Encyclopedia Americana*. New York: 1969.

"The Problem of Metaphor in Translating Walt Whitman's *Leaves of Grass*," in *English Studies Today*. Bern, Switzerland: Francke Verlag, 1961. Pp. 269–80.

"The World of Primal Thought," with Charles T. Davis, in *Whitman the Poet*, edited by John C. Broderick. Belmont, California: Wadsworth Publishing Company, Inc., 1962. Pp. 130–32. [From *Walt Whitman's Poems*, pp. 242–48.]

"Critical Comment on M. Asselineau's Paper," in *Literary History & Literary Criticism: ACTA of the Ninth Congress International Federation for Modern Languages & Literature. Held at New York University, August 23–31, 1963*. New York: New York University Press, 1965. Pp. 61–64.

"William James's Determined Free Will," in *Essays on Determinism in American Literature*, edited by Sydney J. Krause. Kent Studies in English 1. Kent, Ohio: Kent State University Press, 1964. Pp. 67–76.

"Walt Whitman: The Search for a Democratic Structure," in *Discussions of Poetry: Form and Structure*, edited by Francis Murphy. Boston: D. C. Heath and Company, 1964. Pp. 62–76. [From *Walt Whitman Handbook*, pp. 387–409.]

"The Two Poets of *Leaves of Grass*," in *Patterns of Commitment in American Literature*, edited by Marston LaFrance. Toronto: University of Toronto Press, 1967. Pp. 53–72. [Lecture delivered at Carlton University, Ottawa, in 1965.] *The Two Poets of Leaves of Grass*. Westwood, N. J.: The Kindle Press, 1969. 32 pp.

"The Influence of Space on the American Imagination," in *Essays on*

American Literature in Honor of Jay B. Hubbell, edited by Clarence Gohdes. Durham, North Carolina: Duke University Press, 1967. Pp. 329–42.

"William James's *Pragmatism:* A New Name for Some Old Ways of Thinking," in *Landmarks in American Writing,* edited by Hennig Cohen. New York: Basic Books, 1969. [In Voice of America Forum Series.]

"Walt Whitman's Inner Space," in *Memorial Volume to Robert Faner.* Carbondale and Edwardsville: Southern Illinois University Press: *Papers on Language and Literature,* 1969.

"*Walt Whitman's Poems*" (with Charles T. Davis), in *A Century of Whitman Criticism,* edited by Edwin Haviland Miller. Bloomington: Indiana University Press, 1969. Pp. 321–37. [From *Walt Whitman's Poems,* pp. 1–21.]

"The Iconography of Walt Whitman," in *The Artistic Legacy of Walt Whitman: A Tribute to Gay Wilson Allen,* edited by Edwin Haviland Miller. New York: New York University Press, 1970.

II. Articles

"Emancipating Hill Billies," *The Archive* (Duke University), XXXVIII (October, 1925), 9–13.

"Jurgen and Faust: From Heaven through the World to Hell," *The Archive,* XXXVIII (November, 1925), 9–13, 43–44.

"Coffee and Human Felicity" [the eighteenth-century coffee house], *The Archive,* XXXVIII (June, 1926), 5–10.

"The Country Doctor: Reflections on the Rural Medicine Man," *The Archive,* XL (October, 1927), 13–15.

"Jurgen and Faust," *Sewanee Review,* XXXIX (October, 1931), 485–92.

"Biblical Analogies for Walt Whitman's Prosody," *Revue Anglo-Américaine,* X (August, 1933), 490–507.

"Biblical Echoes in Whitman's Works," *American Literature,* VI (November, 1934), 302–15.

"Walt Whitman—Nationalist or Proletarian?" *English Journal,* XXVI (January, 1937), 48–52.

"Walt Whitman and Jules Michelet," *Études Anglaises,* I (May, 1937), 230–37.

"Sidney Lanier as a Literary Critic," *Philological Quarterly,* XVII (April, 1938), 121–38.

"Walt Whitman's 'Long Journey' Motif," *Journal of English and Germanic Philology,* XXXVIII (January, 1939), 76–95.

"Walt Whitman in Contemporary Literature," *Comparative Literature News Letter,* II (December, 1943), 4–5.

"Walt Whitman's Reception in Scandinavia," *Papers of the Bibliographical Society of America,* XL (Fourth Quarter, 1946), 259–75.

"On the Trochaic Meter of 'Pioneers! O Pioneers!' " *American Literature*, XX (January, 1949), 449–51.

"Walt Whitman: Cosmos-Inspired," *New World Writing*, 8th Mentor Selection, 1955, pp. 266–80.

"Whitman Bibliography, 1944–1955," with Evie Allison Allen, *The Walt Whitman Foundation Bulletin*, VIII (April, 1955), 10–34.

"Walt Whitman, *Leaves of Grass* (As broadcast February 13, 1955)," [Gay Wilson Allen, David Daiches, Lyman Bryson], *The Invitation to Learning Reader*, V, No. 1 (1955), 46–54.

"The Young Whitman," *The Youth's Companion* [Tokyo, Japan: The Obunsha Press], December, 1955, pp. 6–9.

"Walt Whitman: Passage to India," *Indian Literature* [New Delhi: Sahitya Akademi (National Academy)], II, No. 2 (April–September, 1959), 38–44. [To be used as an introduction to a translation of *Leaves of Grass* into the eighteen principal languages of India.]

"Carl Sandburg: Fire and Smoke," *The South Atlantic Quarterly*, LIX (Summer, 1960), 315–31.

"Whitman and the Influence of Space on American Literature" [report on a symposium based on this paper, held at the Newberry Library in Chicago, May 5, 1961], *Newberry Library Bulletin*, Vol. V, No. 9 (December, 1961).

"With Faulkner in Japan," *American Scholar* (Autumn, 1962), pp. 566–71.

"Editing the Writings of Walt Whitman: A Million Dollar Project Without a Million Dollars," *Arts and Sciences* [New York University Graduate School of Arts and Science], I, No. 1 (1962/3), 7–12.

"William James: America's Pioneer of Psychical Research" [excerpts from *William James* with additional illustrations], *International Journal of Parapsychology* (March, 1967), pp. 5–31.

III. Reviews

"Humor in America" [Constance Rourke, *American Humor*], *Sewanee Review*, XL (January, 1932), 111–12.

"Whittier's Use of the Bible" [J. S. Stevens, *Whittier's Use of the Bible*], *American Literature*, III (March, 1931), 109–10.

"Schyberg's *Walt Whitman*," *Études Anglaises*, I (May, 1937), 270–71.

"Schyberg's *Dansk Teaterkritik*," *Journal of English and Germanic Philology*, XXXVII (January, 1938), 120–21.

George Leroy White, *Scandinavian Themes in American Literature*, *American Literature*, X (March, 1938), 111–12.

Henry Seidel Canby, *Walt Whitman: An American*, *American Literature*, XV (January, 1944), 423–25.

"Symbols of a Spiritual Rebirth" [article-review on Johannes V. Jensen, who had recently won the Nobel Prize in Literature], *The New York Times Book Review*, April 15, 1945, pp. 4, 28.

"Beulah City, Arizona" [Wilbur Daniel Steele, *That Girl from Memphis*], *The New York Times Book Review*, June 10, 1945, p. 5.

"Amherst Parnassus" [Henry Wells, *Introduction to Emily Dickinson*], *The New York Times Book Review*, July 4, 1948, p. 4.

"The Three Whitmans" [*The Complete Poetry and Prose of Walt Whitman*, edited by Malcolm Cowley], *New Republic* (October 25, 1948), pp. 23–24.

"Whitman Abroad" [translations and foreign criticism], *Comparative Literature*, I (Summer, 1949), 272–77.

"Comprehensive 'Whitman' " [Louis Untermeyer, editor, *The Poetry and Prose of Walt Whitman*], *The New York Times Book Review*, January 1, 1950, p. 10.

"Our Literature Surveyed" [Arthur Hobson Quinn, editor, *The Literature of the American People*], *New York Herald Tribune Book Review*, September 16, 1951, p. 14.

"The Poet and the Personality" [Horace Traubel, *With Walt Whitman in Camden*, Volume IV, and S. Musgrove, *Walt Whitman and T. S. Eliot*], *The New York Times Book Review*, November 29, 1953, p. 24.

Milton Hindus, *Leaves of Grass One Hundred Years After*, *American Literature*, XXVII (November, 1955), 433–34.

"The Flowering of New York" [Perry Miller, *The Raven and the Whale: The War of Words and Wits in the Era of Poe and Melville*], *Saturday Review* (June 23, 1956), pp. 23–24.

Fredson Bowers, *Walt Whitman's Manuscripts*, *Modern Language Quarterly*, XVII (June, 1956), 173–74.

"Whitman in Japan, China, and Finland," *Walt Whitman Newsletter*, III (June, 1957), 26–27.

"Pioneer of Naturalism" [Milton R. Stern, *The Fine Hammered Steel of Herman Melville*, and Merton M. Sealts, Jr., *Melville as Lecturer*], *Saturday Review* (January 11, 1958), pp. 18–19.

James E. Miller, Jr., *A Critical Guide to Leaves of Grass*, *American Literature*, XXX (May, 1958), 250–51.

"Wright Morris on Whitman: A Review" [of *The Territory Ahead*], *Walt Whitman Review*, V (June, 1959), 33–35.

"Uncommon Man in the Service of the Common Good" [Kermit Vanderbilt, *Charles Eliot Norton: Apostle of Culture in Democracy*], *The New York Times Book Review*, September 13, 1959, pp. 6, 42.

"In Literature's Limbo" [Richard B. Hovey, *John Jay Chapman: An American Mind*], *Saturday Review* (November 14, 1959), p. 29.

"Whitman's 1855–56 Notebook" [Harold W. Blodgett, editor, *Walt Whitman: An 1855–56 Notebook Toward the Second Edition of Leaves of Grass*], *Walt Whitman Review*, V (December, 1959), 76–77.

"All Aquiver in Revolt" [Malcolm Cowley, editor, *Walt Whitman's Leaves of Grass: The First (1855) Edition*], *The New York Times Book Review*, February 28, 1960, p. 42.

"Salute to This Century's Fiction" [Willard Thorp, *American Writing in the Twentieth Century*], *Saturday Review* (March 26, 1960), p. 38.

"He sought a World to Fit His Size" [Elizabeth Nowell, *Thomas Wolfe: A Biography*], *Saturday Review* (July 16, 1960), p. 17.

"Loved but Lonely" [Lillian Gilkes, *Cora Crane: A Biography of Mrs. Stephen Crane*], *Saturday Review* (November 19, 1960), pp. 50, 52.

"The Poet Must Be Engaged" [Archibald MacLeish, *Poetry and Experience*], *The New York Times Book Review*, January 8, 1961, p. 6.

"With Walt at the Front" [Walter Lowenfels and Nan Braymer, editors, *Walt Whitman's Civil War*, and Roger Asselineau, *The Evolution of Walt Whitman*], *The New York Times Book Review*, January 22, 1961, p. 3.

"It's All in Our Imagination" [Daniel G. Hoffman, *Form and Fable in American Fiction*], *Saturday Review* (June 3, 1961), p. 39.

"Aloneness" [Edwin T. Bowden, *The Dungeon of the Human Heart*], *Saturday Review* (August 5, 1961), p. 18.

"Red Badge of Suffering" [Louis Zara, *Dark Rider: A Novel Based on the Life of Stephen Crane*], *Saturday Review* (September 23, 1961), p. 18.

"Search for the Affirmative" [Ihab Hassan, *Radical Innocence: Studies in the Contemporary American Novel*], *Saturday Review* (October 21, 1961), p. 27.

"Reality in a Monolithic State" [C. P. Snow and Pamela Hansford Johnson, editors, *Stories from Modern Russia*], *Saturday Review* (April 7, 1962), p. 28.

"The Artistry of a Thinker" [Alfred Kazin, *Contemporaries*], *Saturday Review* (May 5, 1962), p. 21.

Roy Harvey Pearce, *The Continuity of American Poetry*, *American Literature*, XXXIV (May, 1962), 300–301.

"Critic Among Friends" [Glenway Wescott, *Images of Truth: Remembrances and Criticism*], *Saturday Review* (October 6, 1962), pp. 41–42.

"Foibles of an Unwitting Feminist" [Yukio Mishima, *After the Banquet*], *Saturday Review* (February 16, 1963), p. 28.

"Asselineau's Study in English" [Roger Asselineau, *The Evolution of Walt Whitman*, Volumes I and II], *Walt Whitman Review*, IX (March, 1963), 19–20.

"Above the Traffic of His Times" [Daniel Cory, *Santayana: The Later Years: A Portrait with Letters*], *Saturday Review* (November 16, 1963), pp. 40–41.

"A Thistledown Personality" [Leon Edel, editor, *The Diary of Alice James*], *Saturday Review* (September 5, 1964), pp. 25, 28.

"An Iron Hand and a Soft Heart" [Aïda DiPace Donald and David Donald, editors, *Diary of Charles Francis Adams*], *Saturday Review* (November 21, 1964), p. 28.

Darrel Abel, *American Literature, American Literature*, XXXVI (January, 1965), 545–46.

"Songs of Himself" [Horace Traubel, *With Walt Whitman in Camden: April 8–September 14, 1889*, edited by Gertrude Traubel], *Saturday Review* (February 27, 1965), pp. 47–48.

"No Affection at First Sight" [Millicent Bell, *Edith Wharton and Henry James: The Story of Their Friendship*], *Saturday Review* (July 10, 1965), p. 39.

"A Note on Comparing Whitman and Nietzsche" [C. N. Stavrou, *Whitman and Nietzsche: A Comparative Study of Their Thought*], *Walt Whitman Review*, XI (September, 1965), 74–76.

"Wicked Wanderer" [Guillaume Apollinaire, *The Heresiarch and Co*, translated by Rémy Inglis Hall], *Saturday Review* (November 6, 1965), pp. 69–70.

C. N. Stavrou, *Whitman and Nietzsche: A Comparative Study of Their Thought, American Literature*, XXXVII (November, 1965), 333–34.

Harvey Gross, *Sound and Form in Modern Poetry, American Literature*, XXXVII (November, 1965), 350–52.

Irvin Ehrenpreis, editor, *American Poetry: Stratford-upon-Avon Studies 7, American Literature*, XXXVIII (January, 1967), 560–61.

"The 'Blue Book' in Facsimile" [edited by Arthur Golden], *Walt Whitman Review*, XIV (March, 1968), 28–29.

"For Young Readers" [Elisabeth Kyle, *Great Ambitions: A Story of the Early Years of Charles Dickens*; Pearle Hendriksen Schultz, *Sir Walter Scott: Wizard of the North*; Olivia Coolidge, *George Bernard Shaw*; Adrien Stoutenburg and Laura Nelson Baker, *Listen America: A Life of Walt Whitman*; Neal F. Austin, *A Biography of Thomas Wolfe*; James Playsted Wood, *Spunkwater, Spunkwater! A Life of Mark Twain*], *The New York Times Book Review*, June 23, 1968, p. 22.

Hyatt H. Waggoner, *American Poets from the Puritans to the Present, American Literature*, XLI (March, 1969), 111–13.

"Literary Criticism" [George Core, editor, *Southern Fiction Today: Renascence and Beyond*; Richard P. Adams, *Faulkner: Myth and Motion*; Walter Brylowski, *Faulkner's Olympian Laugh: Myth in the Novels*; Paschal Reeves, *Thomas Wolfe's Albatross: Race and Nationality in America*; Jackson J. Benson, *Hemingway: The Writer's Art of Self-Defense*], *Saturday Review* (June 21, 1969), pp. 53–54.

NOTES ON CONTRIBUTORS

OSCAR CARGILL. Professor Emeritus of American Literature and former Head of the All-University Department of English at New York University, he is the author of *Intellectual America* (1941), *The Novels of Henry James* (1961), and *Toward a Pluralistic Criticism* (1965).

ROBERT DUNCAN. A member of the Black Mountain group, he has been one of the most important innovators and conservators in recent American poetry. He is the author of *The Opening of the Field* (1961), *Roots and Branches* (1964), and *Bending the Bow* (1968). In *The Sweetness and Greatness of Dante's Divine Comedy*, he acknowledged his indebtedness to the great Italian poet. Here Mr. Duncan renders homage to his American predecessor.

MAX KOZLOFF. Art critic of *The Nation* and contributing editor of *Artforum*, he is one of the foremost commentators on modern painting, sculpture, and architecture. *Renderings*, a collection of his essays, and his monograph on *Jasper Johns* were published in 1969. He received a Guggenheim Fellowship in 1968 to write a history of modern art criticism.

EDWIN HAVILAND MILLER. Professor Miller is the editor of the five-volume edition of *The Correspondence of Walt Whitman* (1961-1969) and of *A Century of Whitman Criticism* (1969). He is also the author of *Walt Whitman's Poetry: A Psychological Journey* (1968).

NED ROREM. The American master of the art of song, he has created sensitive settings for the poems of Whitman, Roethke, Ashbery, Bishop, and others. He has also composed an opera, *Miss Julie*, as well as many instrumental works. He reveals a sensitive ear for prose in *The Paris Diary of Ned Rorem* (1966), *The New York Diary* (1967), and *Music and People* (1968).

O YOU WHOM I OFTEN AND SILENTLY COME

Walt Whitman

NED ROREM

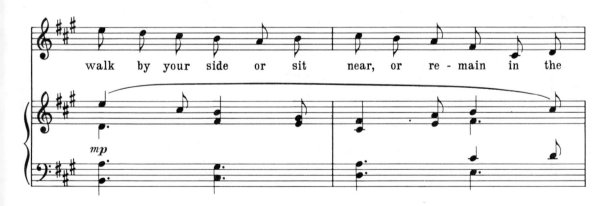

Edition Peters 6284

same room with you,

Lit - tle you know_ the sub - tle e - lec - tric

p

poco rit.

fire_ that for_ your sake is play - ing with - in me._

poco rit.

Hyères, 16 July 57

Edition Peters 6284